P9-AON-585

INTUITION AND SCIENCE

INTUITION AND SCIENCE

Mario Bunge

GREENWOOD PRESS, PUBLISHERS
WESTPORT, CONNECTICUT

Library of Congress Cataloging in Publication Data

Bunge, Mario Augusto.
    Intuition and science.

    Reprint of the ed. published by Prentice-Hall,
Englewood Cliffs, N.J.
        Bibliography: p.
        1. Intuition. 2. Science--Philosophy. I. Ti-
tle.
Q175.B823 1975   501   75-11792
ISBN 0-8371-8066-X

Originally published in 1962 by Prentice-Hall, Inc., Englewood
Cliffs, N.J.

Reprinted with the permission of Prentice-Hall, Inc.

Reprinted in 1975 by Greenwood Press,
a division of Williamhouse-Regency Inc.

Library of Congress Catalog Card Number 75-11792

ISBN 0-8371-8066-X

Printed in the United States of America

Note to the Reader

Most technical terms are explained in the Glossary at the end of the book.

References are given in the footnotes in a sketchy form. Details will be found in the Bibliography.

TABLE OF CONTENTS

INTUITION: AN UNDEPENDABLE
EMBRYO   104
Intuitions and their test   104
"Intuitive" vs. "systematic"   107
The role of intuition in science   109

INTRODUCTION

Few words are as highly ambiguous as "intuition." Its unqualified use is so misleading that its expulsion from the dictionary has been earnestly proposed. But such a procedure would not be practical because the word is firmly entrenched in ordinary and even in technical language, and many new terms would have to be introduced in its place.

In some instances, "intuition" may designate a prerational faculty (sensible intuition); in others a suprarational aptitude (pure intuition, essence intuition, mystic intuition); in still others a variety of reason (intellectual intuition).

Philosophers and scientists do not usually agree on the meaning of "intuition." Among philosophers, intuition, without qualification, is almost always a faculty of the human mind which differs from both sensibility and reason and is no less than an autonomous mode of cognition—namely, sudden, total, and accurate apprehension.

Scientists, on the other hand, are mostly concerned with inferred knowledge, which is mediate, partial, inaccurate, and laboriously elaborated. They are not inclined to believe in immediate apprehension of ready-made ideas and in sudden secure self-evidence but, rather, in more or less rapid constructions and in quick fragmentary inference.

Those who are scientifically oriented—whether in science or in philosophy—may believe in intuitions of various sorts but not in intuitionism. Intuition may be a source of progress when its products—usually rough conjectures—are tested. Intuitionism, on the other hand, is a regressive trend in philosophy, which dogmatically proclaims the existence and even the superiority of an inscrutable and uncontrollable manner of knowing.

Philosophers and scientists alike use the word "intuition," often carelessly. This work attempts to elucidate the functions intuition fulfils in those fields of thought where it occurs most frequently: philosophy, mathematics, and factual science.

The substance of this book was delivered in lectures sponsored by the Departments of Mathematics, Philosophy, and Physics, at the University of Pennsylvania in the fall of 1960. I am grateful to Professor Isaac Schoenberg for having organized them.

I gratefully acknowledge constructive critical remarks by Professors Paul Bernays and Emil Grosswald and my wife Marta. And I thank my student, Mr. Herman Potok, and the editorial staff of Prentice-Hall, for purging the manuscript of its English mistakes.

M.B.

INTUITION AND SCIENCE

1

PHILOSOPHICAL
INTUITIONISM

FROM ARISTOTLE TO KANT

Roots of Aristotelian intuitionism

In his *Organon*,[1] the main logical work of antiquity, Aristotle
(384-321 B.C.) expounds jointly two theses which ought to be
distinguished, although they have almost always been considered as one. They are (1) the *fundamentalist* thesis, according
to which every branch of knowledge has a foundation or point
of departure which is both *radical* (ultimate and final) and
absolute, i.e., independent of the way in which the subject in
question is approached and expounded; and (2) the *infallibilist*
thesis, according to which every piece of knowledge deserving
to be called scientific must be *secure* and *incorrigible*, to which
end it must be based on premises that need not be demonstrated and are undoubtedly true and *self-evident*.

Fundamentalism and infallibilism are certainly not peculiar
to the Aristotelian system alone but are, rather, characteristic
of dogmatism in general, be it idealist, empiricist, or material-
ist. Both can be found, for instance, in the demand of founding
"secure knowledge" on what is immediately given in sensation
(sensism), and in the requirement of founding it on allegedly
eternal principles of pure reason (classical rationalism). Need-
less to say, the progress of knowledge, which consists partly in
revising and expanding whatever is taken as known and proved,
has discredited both fundamentalism and infallibilism. Every

[1] Aristotle, *Organon, Posterior Analytics*, Book I, chapter ii.

1

foundation is now regarded as perfectible, and every statement about things and events as corrigible.

Now, a proposition that is taken as a premiss in a given context is undemonstrable in that context. And if it is not granted that such premisses (axioms or postulates) may be tentatively stated as hypotheses (factual science) or as conventions (formal science), how could they be established except by induction or intuition? But induction, which Aristotle regards as the method whereby even sensible perception "implants the universal," does not yield secure knowledge,[2] as is evidenced by the failure of most of our empirical generalizations; and insecure knowledge is not scientific according to infallibilism. Therefore, intuition remains as the only mode of apprehension of the premisses of scientific discourse. Ultimately, "intuition will be the originative source of scientific knowledge." [3]

Fundamentalism and infallibilism, then, lead to intuitionism. Or rather—in the case of Aristotle and of many others who grant the value of sensible experience and of deduction—they lead to postulating the existence of intuition as an autonomous mode of knowing and as the supreme source of truth. Unfortunately, the very *existence* of such a capacity for the global and sudden apprehension of secure knowledge is not thereby established.

Intuition, which occupied a marginal place in Aristotelian philosophy, has been assigned an important role in modern philosophy.

Descartes' rational intuition

The same quest for ultimate foundation and for certainty impels Descartes (1596-1650)—much more peripatetic than he thinks, although he is the founder of modern philosophy—to propose that we employ nothing but intuition and deduction, for only by these means shall we attain the knowledge of things without fear of error.[4]

[2] *Ibid.*, Book II, chapter xix, 100b.
[3] *Ibid.*
[4] Descartes, *Règles pour la direction de l'esprit*, III, *Oeuvres*, Vol. 11.

For Descartes intuition consists in "the conception of an attentive spirit, so distinct and clear that no doubt remains in him about that which he understands; or, that which is the same, the conception of a sound and attentive spirit, a conception born in the light of reason alone, and which is more certain because it is simpler than deduction itself." [5] Cartesian intuition is, then, a *rational* operation whereby certain truths are presented in a total and immediate way; and these self-evident propositions are to be chosen as axioms.

Among the propositions that "must be seen intuitively" Descartes mentions "$2 + 2 = 4$," "$3 + 1 = 4$," and their consequence, namely, "$2 + 2 = 3 + 1$." We are to understand intuitively—that is, without analysis—that this last is a necessary consequence of the former two,[6] as well as the general principle involved, viz., "Two things equal to a third one are equal to each other" (i.e., the transitivity of equality).[7]

According to Descartes, man has no other way for attaining the certain knowledge of truth, except through self-evident intuition and necessary demonstration.[8] And such knowledge is the sole type he ought to procure; merely probable or insecure knowledge is to be rejected. "We must concern ourselves with nothing but the objects about which our mind seems capable of acquiring knowledge both certain and indubitable," he writes as if echoing Plato (c. 427-347 B.C.) and his dichotomy of *episteme* (science) and *doxa* (opinion).[9]

Here again, at the dawn of modern philosophy, fundamentalism and infallibilism, the search for an *episteme* regarded as knowledge based upon immovable principles and data, leads to intuitionism, just as in other cases it has led to sensist empiricism. But Cartesian intuitionism is, like the Aristotelian, of a moderate sort, for it conceives of intuition as a rational

[5] *Ibid.*, Rule III.
[6] *Ibid.*
[7] *Ibid.*, Rule XII.
[8] *Ibid.*, Rules III and XII.
[9] *Ibid.*, Rule II.

4 PHILOSOPHICAL INTUITIONISM

operation and it insists that "intelligence alone is capable of conceiving the truth." [10]

Besides, for Descartes fundamentalism and infallibilism go hand in hand with the fight against scholasticism, the aim of which was not precisely to deal with objects "about which our mind seems capable of acquiring knowledge both certain and indubitable." The plea for "clear and distinct ideas" was a battle cry against obscurantism with its unintelligible and empty verbosity. Revelation, authority, pure reason, and ordinary experience had been discredited by the schoolmen. Scientific experience on the one hand, and intuition on the other, were to be valued by the new thinkers.

We are still far from the contemporary anti-intellectual intuitionism of a Bergson, a Scheler, or a Heidegger. Yet it was that same moderate intuitionism inherent in classical rationalism (Descartes, Spinoza, Leibniz) which was developed by Kant and which ended in the case of most Romantics and contemporary irrationalists, from Schelling to Heidegger, by swallowing reason altogether.

Any student of mathematics might nowadays refute the naïve intuitionism of Descartes, by disputing the intuitive character of the propositions he used as examples. Descartes could not know that ordinary arithmetic is one among an infinity of conceivable arithmetical systems, including, among others, the calculus used for counting hours and measuring angles, in which strange equalities, such as "$12 + 1 = 1$" and "$360 + 1 = 1$" are found. In alternative number systems—for instance, those accepting negative numbers only—a proposition such as "$2 + 2 = 4$" is not even meaningful, since such numbers simply do not exist in these contexts. Such noncanonical arithmetics may not seem "intuitive" to those who are not used to them.

The transitivity of equality was another Cartesian intuition. Yet Piaget has shown that the notion of transitivity is acquired along with the logical organization of thought, and is absent in the prelogical or intuitive schematization that characterizes

[10] *Ibid.*, Rule XII.

the early years of life. According to Piaget, "at intuitive levels the subject declines to derive from the two perceptually verified inequalities A < B and B < C the conclusion A < C." [11] But, of course, Descartes lived in an era when genetic, evolutionary thought did not prevail.

Nor could Descartes know that the transitivity he invoked is a property of *formal* equality, not necessarily of other types of equivalence, such as perceptual equality. In fact, it often happens that we are not able to discriminate differences between two sensible objects A and B, nor between B and a third one C and say, "Evidently A is equal to B, and B is equal to C." Yet we may distinguish A from C as the result of the accumulation of the imperceptible differences between A and B, and between B and C, in such a way that their sum surpasses the perceptual threshold. A being endowed with an infinite perceptual acuteness might not find two identical material things, so that the famous axiom mentioned by Descartes as intuitively valid ("Two things equal to a third one are equal to each other") would not be used by him outside the field of concepts. But we need not resort to this fiction. The microscope, which came into wide use a little after Descartes wrote, showed that many equalities were only apparent.

Once we recognize the weakness of sensible intuition (the source of our judgments of perception), the pitfalls of abbreviated reasonings, and the relative character of mathematical truth, how can we still believe in the existence of Cartesian intuition as a source of certainty?

Spinoza's intuitive science

Spinoza (1632-1677) distinguished more levels in cognitive activity than did Descartes. He listed knowledge of the first kind (be it of individual physical objects or of signs), reason or knowledge of the second kind, and a third kind of cognition, the *scientia intuitiva:* "And this kind of knowledge proceeds from the adequate idea of the formal essence of certain attri-

[11] Piaget, *The Psychology of Intelligence* (1950), p. 134. Used by permission.

butes of God [Nature] to the adequate knowledge of the essence
of things." [12] The supreme virtue of the soul "is to understand
things by the third kind of knowledge." [13]

The instance of intuitive knowledge provided by Spinoza is,
again, of a logico-mathematical kind. It would occur in the
solution of the following problem: Given three integers, find
a fourth which would be to the third as the second is to the
first. We usually resort to a rule learned at school, namely,
$a:b::c:x, \therefore x = bc:a$. But, according to Spinoza, if the given
numbers are simple, such as 1,2, and 3, "nobody can fail to
see that the fourth proportional is 6, and this the more clearly
so since from the very relation which—as we see at a glance
—the 1st holds to the 2nd, we conclude the 4th." [14] How do we
conclude? By multiplying by 2, or by remembering that twice
3 is 6 (since the relation we grasp is "twice"). And this operation is so quick for any literate adult person that it presents
itself as a flash of intuition.

We realize what Spinoza's intuition is: just quick inference,
usually aided by the sight of signs (physical marks) representing
the concepts involved. Leibniz (1646-1716), the third giant of
the rationalist trilogy, will not conceive intuition otherwise.
Yet neither Spinoza nor Leibniz faced up to the paradox that
intuition, regarded by them as the highest mode of cognition,
was insufficient for the establishment of any basic new principle
of mathematics or factual science.

Kant's pure intuition

Kant (1724-1804) seems to have adapted the Spinozan trichot-
omy of spiritual activity. In addition to sensible (empirical)
intuition and understanding, Kant introduces pure intuition
(*reine Anschauung*). The principles of this a priori, superaem-
pirical sensibility are dealt with by the transcendental aesthetic,
a discipline which establishes that "there are two pure forms of

[12] Spinoza, *Ethics*, Part II, Proposition XL, Schol. II.
[13] *Ibid.*, Part V, Prop. XXV.
[14] *Ibid.*, Part II, Prop. XL, Schol. II.

sensible intuition, serving as principles of a priori knowledge, namely, space and time." [15] "Space is a necessary a priori representation, which underlies all outer intuitions" [16]; in particular, in order to perceive a thing, we must be in the possession of the a priori notion of space. Nor is time an empirical concept: it is the form of the inner sense, and "is a necessary representation that underlies all intuitions." [17]

Pure intuition, unaided by the senses and, moreover, constituting the very possibility of sense experience, is for Kant the source of all synthetic a priori judgments. These include the synthetic judgments of geometry, which is for Kant the a priori science of physical space, and arithmetic, which he regards as based on counting, a process that takes time. Moreover, if for Aristotle, Descartes and Spinoza intuition was a mode of knowing first truths, it is for Kant no less than the possibility of outer experience.

We now know what remains of the a priori, necessary, absolute, and self-evident character assigned by Kant to the axioms of mathematics. We grant that they are a priori—as the idealists had pointed out, and as some empiricists had admitted—but not that they are absolutely necessary and, even less, self-evident. We have many geometries none of which are logically necessitated, since they are all consistent with one and the same system of logic. The history of science shows us how laborious, how far from the easy intuitive grasp, has been man's process of building those concepts and theories which he has invented in the last few millenia.

Contemporary geometries may be classed into three species: (*a*) mathematical geometries, both abstract, i.e., uninterpreted, and concrete, i.e., interpreted in terms of points, lines, surfaces, etc.; (*b*) physical geometries true to various approximations (such as the relativistic theories of spacetime); (*c*) perceptual geometries, i.e., theories of visual, auditory, tactile, and muscu-

[15] Kant, *Kritik der reinen Vernunft*, B 35-36, Kemp-Smith translation.
[16] *Ibid.*, B 38.
[17] *Ibid.*, B 46.

lar spaces. Psychologists have taught us that Euclidean geometry —the only geometrical theory known to Kant, although projective geometry had been born more than one century before —is not the most natural one from the psychologistic point of view adopted by Kant. In fact, visual space—the space constituted by the relations among the objects of normal vision —is inhomogeneous and anisotropic, and seems to fit the non-Euclidean, hyperbolic geometry of Lobachevski.[18]

We know, too, that mathematical judgments, though a priori, are analytic and not synthetic, in the sense that they are justifiable by purely logical means. And we have learned to distinguish the infinitely many possible mathematical geometries from the physical geometry we adopt at every stage in research. As to the axioms of most of these geometries, they have become so complex that nobody could consider them self-evident or suprarational. Only their lack of self-evidence is evident. Witness the form that the generalized Pythagorean theorem takes on in Riemannian geometry: $ds^2 = \Sigma\ g_{ik}\ dg^i\ dg^k$, which, incidentally, has the logical status of an axiom in this theory.

The "faculty" by means of which man creates (or constructs, or produces) geometries and theories is reason—certainly sustained in some cases by sensible intuition, though not by any mysterious pure intuition. However, the products of reason are not all of them self-evident and definitive.

Kantian time had a similar fate. We now consider that the characterization of time as the a priori form of the inner sense is psychologistic, and we reject the radical separation between time and physical space. The theories of relativity have taught us that the concepts of physical space and time are neither a priori nor independent from one another and from the concepts of matter and field.

Infallibilism is, of course, one of the sources of Kantian intuitionism. Further sources are psychologism and the correct

---

[18] Luneburg, *Mathematical Analysis of Binocular Vision* (1947).

acknowledgment that sensible experience is insufficient for building categories (e.g., the category of space). Instead of supposing that man builds concepts which enable him to understand the raw experience he—like other animals—has, without such *entia rationis*, Kant holds dogmatically and, as we now know, in opposition to contemporary animal and child psychology, that "outer experience is possible only by the representation that has been thought." [19]

Of all the influential contributions of Kant, his idea of pure intuition has proved to be the least valuable, but not, unfortunately, the least influential.

CONTEMPORARY INTUITIONISM

If Cartesian and Spinozan intuitions are *forms* of reason, Kantian intuition *transcends* reason, and this is why it constitutes the germ of contemporary intuitionism, in turn a gateway to irrationalism. There are, to be sure, important differences. While Kant admitted the value of sensible experience and of reason, which he regarded as insufficient but not as impotent, contemporary intuitionists tend to revile both. Whereas Kant fell into intuitionism because he realized the limitation of sensibility and the exaggerations of traditional rationalism, and because he misunderstood the nature of mathematics, intuitionists nowadays do not attempt to solve a single serious *problem* with the help of either intuition or its concepts; rather, they are anxious to eliminate intellectual problems, to cut down reason and planned experience, and to fight rationalism, empiricism, and materialism.

This anti-intellectualist brand of intuitionism grew during the Romantic period (roughly, the first half of the nineteenth century) directly from the Kantian seed, but it did not exert a substantial influence until the end of the century, when it

---

[19] Kant, *op. cit.*, B 38.

ceased being a sickness of isolated professors and became a disease of culture.

Dilthey's "Verstehen"

A typical representative of the intuitionist reaction against science, logic, rationalism, empiricism, and materialism, is Wilhelm Dilthey (1833-1911). In his *Introduction to the Sciences of Spirit* (1883), this erudite-without-ideas maintains that the goal of the sciences of spirit (*Geisteswissenschaften*) must be the grasping of the singular and the total, and that such an apprehension is given in life experience (*Erlebnis*) alone, never as theory.

History, which aims primarily at the literary presentation of unique events in the past, requires a "sympathetic sensibility" (*Mitempfindung*),[20] just as generalization—which is improper for the sciences of spirit—demands a rational effort. And psychology, commands Dilthey, must be conceived as a science of spirit and not as a natural science, in the way the psycho-physicists had conceived it. Moreover, psychology should remain within the bounds of a descriptive discipline which ascertains and "understands" facts, in contradistinction to explanatory (*erklärende*) psychology, which "tries to deduce the whole of spiritual life from certain hypotheses."[21] Only such a psychology of "understanding" (*Verstehen*), based upon the resemblance between other people's experiences and our own, may yield a secure foundation for the sciences of spirit. Ordinary psychology does nothing but pile hypothesis upon hypothesis.[22]

Notice that here, too, the aim is the achievement of "scientific certainty," of "self-evidence in thinking."[23] To this end we must obviously restrict ourselves to individual or particular

[20] Dilthey, *Einleitung in die Geisteswissenschaften*, Book I, chapter xiv (titled "The Philosophy of History and Sociology are not True Sciences"), Vol. I of *Gesammelte Werke*, p. 91.
[21] *Ibid.*, p. 32.
[22] *Ibid.*, pp. 32-3.
[23] *Ibid.*, p. 45.

judgments in the field of the sciences of man, in which not "the mere force of intelligence" but "the power of personal life" renders the best fruits.[24] (Unfortunately Dilthey does not explain what he means by "the power of personal life.") In other words, no generalization, such as the statement of a law, must be looked for in connection with man's individual or social behavior. Such is the barren fruit—to continue the fruit analogy—of infallibilism.

That the demand for "understanding" is unscientific, is clear. Science, despite the efforts of some metascientists, does not try to reduce the new and strange to the old and familiar; it does not propose to "understand" the nonvulgar in common-sense terms. On the contrary, science constructs theoretical concepts and systems which, by *transcending* ordinary experience and common sense, enable us to unify, explain, and predict—in short, account for—whatever, at the level of common sense, appears to be radically diverse, mysterious—though obvious upon occasion—and unpredictable. Science, especially psychology, far from attempting to "understand" reality in terms of ordinary knowledge, explains it in terms of laws describing the relations among increasingly abstract and refined concepts. Most of these concepts are not found in presystematic or intuitive thinking; suffice to recall the explanation of the blue of the sky by molecular physics, or of psychoses by psychochemistry.

Common sense is for science a starting point and a problem: sense data and ordinary judgment are the raw materials which science processes, transcends, and explains—very often *away*. The kind of understanding offered by the "humanist" school in the sciences of man, like common sense and religious explanation, consists of examples and metaphors, individual cases and parables. Its aim is "to bring home" the unknown, remote, unfamiliar, and complex, in terms of the known, immediate, familiar, and simple. Science, far from seeking such a trivialization of problems and explanations, attempts to explain the

[24] *Ibid.*, p. 38.

familiar and yet unexplained in terms of unfamiliar but understandable concepts and propositions.[25]

Notwithstanding the barrenness of the *Verstehen* "method," Dilthey's opinions had some echo, probably because the tide of the hatred of reason was mounting in Europe at that time. His opinions were not fruitful in the *sciences* of man, but they found followers in other fields. In the first place, the movement of the *Geisteswissenschaften* and, particularly, the campaign in favor of that mysterious empathy, or sympathetic understanding (*Einfühlung, Mitempfindung*), were used by pseudoscience and semiscience. Thus, for instance, Freud, Adler, and Jung, maintained that empathy is the highest mode of knowing. And Nazi Germany—which, like California, was incredibly fertile in pseudosciences—prized Dilthey's opposition to science, to "the Anglo-French school" (positivistic and analytic), and to the "liberal dogmas," as well as his exaltation of totality, life, and the State.

Bergson's "metaphysical intuition"

Enormously more refined and interesting representatives of philosophical intuitionism were Bergson, Husserl, and William James. But the activistic and ultilitarian intuitionism of James (1842-1910), so different because of its dynamicism from the contemplative intuitionism of Husserl, derives largely from Bergsonian intuitionism, so that we may omit it in this rapid glance.[26]

Intuition is for Bergson (1859-1941) "that kind of *intellectual sympathy* by which one is transported into the interior of an object to coincide with what is unique and consequently ineffable about it." [27] Intuition enables us to grasp whatever remains external to intelligence: movement, change in general, life, spirit, history and, above all, "the absolute"—which, of course, is that which is not relative. Intuition is nothing but a highly evolved form of instinct. It is superior to reason in that

[25] See Bunge, *Causality* (1959), chapter 11.
[26] See James, *A Pluralistic Universe* (1909), Lecture VI.
[27] Bergson, "Introduction à la métaphysique" (1903), p. 4.

it expresses itself in categorical form, whereas reason expresses itself in the hypothetical mode.[28] How could we doubt that instinct is higher than reason, if the former can decidedly assert (and even shout) "*q*," whereas the latter only dares to state "*q* on condition that *p*," *i.e.*, "if *p* then *q*"?

Intelligence, according to Bergson, accounts properly for the "inorganic solid" alone and, in general, it is made for the purpose of dealing with inanimate matter. Only instinct leads us to the interior of life, to grasp the unique and universal *élan* (a reprint of the Greek *pneuma*) which moves and enlivens everything. Intelligence, which can clearly represent to itself only the discontinuous, static and old, is incapable of grasping continuity, movement and novelty, which instinct alone recognizes.

The function of the intellect is practical rather than theoretical; and, being an instrument for action, it remains on the surface of things without revealing their nature. Intuition, on the other hand, is "instinct turned disinterested and, aware of itself, is able to reflect on its object and is capable of amplifying it unlimitedly." [29]

What is intuitively given, says Bergson, can be expressed in either of two ways: by the image or by the concept. The development of intuition is conceptual, but the nucleus of every system of ideas, such as a philosophical system, is an original intuition that must be grasped.[30] Thus philosophy is, for Bergson, the opposite of analysis: it does not try to decompose, separate, and discriminate—this being the menial work of intelligence, which is essentially superficial; the proper task of philosophy is to trace back the original simplicity engendered by intuition. This task is accomplished by metaphysics directly, without the symbols that characterize conceptual thought.[31]

Bergson's intuition is not knowledge proper and is recognized by him as nebulous. It would be nothing without the stirrings

---

[28] Bergson, *L'évolution créatrice* (1907), p. 150.
[29] *Ibid.*, p. 178.
[30] Bergson, "L'intuition philosophique" (1911).
[31] Bergson, "Introduction à la métaphysique" (1903), p. 4.

of intelligence; without intelligence, intuition would still be
pure instinct focusing on the moving singular.[32] But intuition
takes things from the inside—as Hegel wanted reason to do
—and yields a certainty of which reason is utterly incapable.
The quest for certainty and for ultimate foundations is, once
again, the main source of intuitionism.

Bergson enumerates with prolixity what he regards as limitations of reason, but he does not care to *prove* that intuition is
a mode of cognition higher than reason. Among the few illustrations of the fertility of intuition he mentions the second
law of thermodynamics, of which he knows a formulation in
ordinary language. (The law of increasing entropy was very
popular in Bergson's time.) The example was not wisely chosen.
The law in question had required much rational and empirical
work; its various statements are difficult to understand without
the help of experiments and formulas; and it lends itself to
many different interpretations. In short, the law is far from
being intuitive and self-evident. The second postulate of
thermodynamics has been phrased in various anthropomorphic
ways, such as "Energy becomes progressively degraded," "Everything deteriorates in time," "The universe is running down,"
and "The ultimate fate of the universe is thermal death." But
surely science cannot be blamed if some of its vulgarizations
serve as fodder for antiscientific philosophers.

Besides, does not Bergson contradict himself when he maintains that the function of the intellect is not theoretical but
practical? Are not theories conceptual systems? Are not theories,
such as thermodynamics and genetics, the work of reason and
of experience, guided by hypotheses? And are not scientific
theories, in contrast to intuitive representations, characterized
by minimal vagueness and ambiguity? Certainly pure reason
alone is insufficient to build scientific theory. Empirical information and the various forms of genuine intuition—with the
exception of metaphysical, essential, and mystical intuition—
are essential ingredients in the process of theory construction.

[32] Bergson, *L'évolution créatrice* (1907), p. 179.

But intuition is, in this case, either a form of reason or its tool (see Chapter 3); furthermore, it does not occur in the final exposition of the theory.

It sounds strange that Bergson should have maintained that the intellect is incapable of grasping even the simplest sort of change, namely, mechanical motion. Does not natural science, and particularly physics, deal with change? The ground of that remarkable belief, shared by James, seems to be that conceptual thinking cannot apprehend becoming, because concepts are static and are isolated among one another. This argument, which had been employed by Hegel (1770-1831) against formal logic, ignores the fact that science creates not only concepts of invariable classes, but also variables (e.g., "reaction velocity," "rate of growth," "acceleration") capable of describing changing aspects of experience. The argument also ignores the fact that every proposition *relates* concepts, so that the latter are never piled up as isolated bricks.

The differential and integral calculus was invented partly in order to elucidate in an exact way the rough (preanalytic, intuitive) concepts of instantaneous velocity and acceleration; they provided concepts (numerical variables) that could faithfully represent the instantaneous state and the evolution of material systems of any kind. (This does not mean, of course, that calculus is "the mathematics of change," as has so often been held. Every theory of material change is a factual, not a formal theory, and if mathematical formulas occur in such a theory, it is alongside certain rules of designation and/or interpretive postulates specifying the meaning of symbols. Thus, the formula "$v = ds/dt$" does not enter physics until the meanings of the variables "s" and "t" have been specified, which can be done in an unlimited number of ways. For instance, "s" may denote distance, volume, concentration, charge, etc., and "t" may stand for time, angular position, and so on.)

Most of the variables of physics, chemistry, physiology, and psychology are continuous, notwithstanding Bergson's belief that the sciences of matter do not grasp continuity. We are so used to continuity that, when quantum mechanics was first proposed, some conservative scientists rejected it because it made room for certain discontinuities: they maintained that such jumps were not "intuitive." (Even Schroedinger, one of the originators of the quantum theory, preferred to speak of frequency changes without specifying what they were frequencies of; and Planck sought all his life to explain quantization in terms of continuous mechanical motions.) Hilbert, the formalist, believed that continuity is intuitive; Brouwer, the intuitionist mathematician, thinks that what is intuitively given is the sequence of discrete units. Is there an ultimate tribunal to decide which concept is *inherently* the more intuitive? Or is the question itself meaningless, intuitability being relative to the subject and his background?

As to qualitative novelty, which Bergson and the emergentists held to be rationally unexplainable, do not nuclear physics, chemistry, evolution theory, psychology, sociology, and so many other scientific theories account for it? It is true that scientists and metascientists can be found who, in the name of the unity of science, will deny the emergence of radical novelty; but the demonstration that the new is *reducible* to the old is always a chicane: it consists in showing that the new can be *explained* as a product of the old.

No chemist seriously believes—unless he is at the moment trying to defend an anachronistic mechanistic cosmology or an inadequate theory of scientific explanation, such as the reduction of the unfamiliar to the familiar—that water is somehow contained in hydrogen and oxygen separately, or that the properties of water are merely apparent, only those of its constituents being real. And no biologist denies the emergence of new traits in the course of evolution; on the contrary, his problem is to give a lawful account of a wealth of variety and change. Scientists try to frame rational and testable explanations of the emergence of novelty; that such explanations may seem mysterious to those who do not care to study them, is not a sign of the impotence of reason.

Bergson's critique of intelligence would have been timely if it had concerned medieval science; as it was, it came three centuries too late. What is worse, the medicine he offered was no better than the sickness. He did not recommend that we develop our intelligence but, on the contrary, suggested that we subject it to a "faculty" devoid of those powers of logical systematization and grounded criticism which are characteristic of modern culture.

Husserl's "Wesensschau"

In his *Ideas* (1913), influential in German-speaking countries, Latin America, and post-occupation France, Husserl (1859-1938) revived the Platonic and Aristotelian essentialism that looks for the immutable essence of things beyond their properties and laws. Moreover, Husserl claims that such an essence or *eidos* is given by a special faculty, namely, the intellectual (but not rational) intuition he calls "vision of essences" (*Wesensschau*).

Empirical or individual intuition, and essential or universal intuition (since it is supposed to apprehend universality), are the sources of the ultimate justification of every judgment,[33] even if the original intuition is not altogether adequate, in which case it will require certain transformations. These operations, the phenomenological reduction or *epoche,* the "eidetic variation," etc., are as many purification rites that remind us of the preliminary acts by means of which Bacon (1561-1626) wished us to get rid of the *idola* before marrying that chaste old lady, Observation. The phenomenological rites, too, are supposed to remove from our minds the burden of presuppositions.

The knowledge of essences, or eidetic knowledge, is inde-

---

[33] Husserl, *Ideen zu einer reinen Phänomenologie und phänomenologischen Philosophie* (1913), Book I, chapter i, in *Husserliana,* Vol. III.

pendent of factual knowledge even when it deals with the essence of material objects. Furthermore, it does not presuppose the real existence of the object, which must be suspended or "bracketed." This operation is indispensable in order to protect phenomenology from empirical refutation. Since eidetic truths assert nothing about facts, no truth of fact can be deduced from them and, as a consequence, such "truths" cannot be confirmed or disconfirmed by empirical investigation.[34] Phenomenology, even if it is about the world, is above the world.

Eidetic judgments, the products of the vision of essences or eidetic intuition, are then a priori synthetic judgments having, over the Kantian ones, the clear advantage of being altogether irrelevant to experience and almost unintelligible. They are reputed to be true independently of ordinary experience. As Scheler explains, "the essences and their connections are 'given' *before* any experience of this kind [i.e., ordinary experience], that is, they are given a priori; on the other hand, the propositions that find their fulfilment in them are 'true' a priori." [35] "That which is intuited as an essence or as a connection among such essences cannot, as a consequence, be nullified either by observation or by induction, and cannot be improved or perfected." [36] The truths of phenomenology are, in contradistinction to those of science, definitive.

Phenomenology offers, then, the means for satisfying the requirements of fundamentalism and infallibilism. On the one hand, the reduction to pure consciousness operates as a means for attaining the root of things, for rendering both a "return to the things themselves" and an "absolute beginning" possible. On the other hand, the *Wesensschau* originates the *reine Wesenswissenschaften* (pure sciences of essences), or eidetic sciences, which allegedly exhibit the laws of essences (*Wesensgesetze*) and serve as an immovable foundation for the posi-

[34] *Ibid.*, #4.
[35] Scheler, *Der Formalismus in der Ethik und die materiale Wertethik* (1916), pp. 69-70.
[36] *Ibid.*, p. 70.

tive, or empirical sciences—even though scientists seem unaware of this.

That infallibilism, the quest for what Husserl calls "apodictic evidence," and fundamentalism are springs of phenomenological intuitionism, is clear. "Genuine science and the genuine lack of prejudice which characterizes it requires as a basis [*Unterlage*] of all demonstrations, judgments immediately valid as such, or deriving their validity directly from source [*originär gebenden*] intuitions." [37] Adequate intuitions are altogether *indubitable:* they have, according to Husserl, the same apodictic character as the judgments of science. [38] The certainty that the radical empiricist assigns to the protocol or observational statement and that the traditional rationalist finds in the innate idea or the immutable principle of reason, is assigned by Husserl to an intuition that "sees things themselves," that apprehends no less than the immutable essence without paying attention to annoying trifles such as existence or empirical corroboration.

Phenomenology does not bar doubt in general, but confines it to the data of experience and to the empirical sciences, which can afford uncertainty, since they are second-class subjects. On the other hand, the intuition of essences cannot be doubted, although Husserl does not offer examples showing the actual *existence* of that faculty, of an a priori, extraempirical and suprarational grasping of essences; nor does he prove that there are essences *beyond* the properties and relations studied by science, i.e., in some Platonic realm of eternal Ideas.

Equally uncertain remains Husserl's claim that the "eidetic sciences"—which he mentions as possible, but which he does not care to build—have actually been the foundation of a single science of facts. [39] It could not be argued that this is the case

---

[37] Husserl, *op. cit.* p. 43. See also *Cartesianische Meditationen* (1931), ##3, 5, 6.

[38] Husserl, *Cartesianische Meditationen* (1931), #6.

[39] See Zilsel, "Phenomenology and Natural Science" (1941); Margenau, "Phenomenology and Physics" (1944); and Bunge, "La fenomenología y la ciencia" (1951).

with logic and mathematics (which are eidetic sciences according to Husserl). First, these disciplines exist independently of phenomenology and have evolved in a direction opposed to Husserl's wishes. (It may be recalled that he ridiculed Frege's attempt to base mathematics on logic[40] and that he remained altogether outside the movement of renewal of logic, in which Frege, Peano, Whitehead, and Russell took part.) Second, logic and mathematics are instruments rather than "bases" of factual science. Perhaps in some sense it is true that, at a given moment, an empirical datum forms a part of the "basis" of science (that is, while it is not corrected); but to say that formal science, which provides ideal *forms,* constitutes the basis of factual science is like saying that grammar is the basis of poetry, or that brush manufacture is the basis of painting. Third, formal science does not deal with essences in the Husserlian sense. No mathematician asks what the essence of the circle or of the Riemann integral is, and some of the branches of mathematics—its abstract theories—do not even specify the nature of their objects.

Let us clarify the last point, which is important for an appraisal of essentialism. In abstract algebra, for instance, one does not necessarily ask *what* are the entities A and B that satisfy the relation "$AB + BA = 0$." Nobody will seek the "essence" of A and B outside the relation or law "$AB + BA = 0$" that specifies them in an ambiguous way. The essential, in algebra as well as in physics, is the *law* itself, which may be satisfied (if universal) by an infinity of entities. And this law does not spring out of some vision of essences but is built by the mathematician in a manner which is not necessary—as it ought to be were it true that, once the essence of an expression is grasped, it becomes evident that the proposition is necessary (as phenomenology claims). Only mathematical and logical *proofs* are necessary, in the sense that, if they do not fit certain patterns, they are invalid; but the axioms of formal science are not logically necessary.

---

[40] Husserl, *Philosophie der Arithmetik* (1891).

Modern science has abandoned the essentialism of Plato and Aristotle. It does not look after essences conceived as entities and, even less, as entities transcending the objects themselves. On the other hand, science is capable of inventing and discovering laws that are essential in some respect or in some context, even though in some other respect or context they have to be regarded as derivative.

It would be interesting if phenomenologists could show that, besides essential laws, they can point to pure, detached essences and, moreover, to essences grasped by the inner vision of essences. Unfortunately, their writings are characteristically dogmatic and sterile, besides being obscure enough to make room for the widely divergent interpretations of disciples, who from Scheler and Heidegger to Sartre and Merleau-Ponty share nothing but obscurity.[41] As the mathematician von Mises once said, Husserl built a method for seeing things, but he saw nothing with it.[42]

Intuitions of values and norms

Let us finally recall the axiological and ethical intuitionism maintained by David Ross (1877-   ), by semi-phenomenologists like Max Scheler (1874-1928) and Nicolai Hartmann (1882-1950), and by empiricists like George Edward Moore (1873-1958).

According to these philosophers, good and evil, as well as our duties, are known directly and, furthermore, are not analyzable. The basic propositions of ethics and of the theory of value are intuitable (by all or by the privileged), indemonstrable, and irrefutable by experience. Thus, Scheler claimed that there exists an emotional intuition which grasps irrational essences (values)[43], and Moore held that "good," which he regarded as

---

[41] Husserl's own original intention, though, was definitely antidogmatic. He did not realize that by altogether rejecting rationalism and empiricism and by espousing fundamentalism and embarking in the search for certainty, he would inaugurate a new dogma.

[42] von Mises, *Positivism* (1951), p. 277.

[43] Scheler, *Der Formalismus in der Ethik und die materiale Wertethik* (1916), *passim*.

the nuclear concept of ethics, is indefinable, and that nothing but intuition can tell us what things or qualities are good.[44]

Ethical and axiological intuitionism, basically absolutistic, antinaturalistic and antianalytic as it is, refuses to explain and elucidate (for instance in psychological, sociological, or historical terms) ethical words, norms, and judgments, as well as value judgments, and denies the possibility of justifying them or providing a foundation for them, whether empirically or rationally. It thereby erects an irreducible duality between fact and value, between nature and society, between needs, desires and ideals, on the one side, and patterns of moral conduct on the other. Such a dualism bars every attempt to explain, ground and correct, on the basis of experience and reason, both valuational attitudes and moral patterns.[45] It throws human behavior to the thoughtless impulse of the individual or to the will of the "enlightened" one who attributes to himself the possession of a peculiar "intuition of values" or "insight into norms." In this way, ethical and axiological intuitionism favor authoritarianism, that conspicuous shadow of intuitionism.[46]

Naturalists and rationalists, on the other hand, tend to hold that humans are entitled to know *why* work is good and war is bad and what *justifies* a rule such as "Enlighten thy neighbor." Such a goal can be attained by an *analysis* of value judgments and norms and is capable of being pursued despite Moore's branding of any such analyses as instances of what he called "the naturalistic fallacy." An analysis of value will show that, far from being absolute, it is relative. Whatever is valuable (or disvaluable) to some extent is so in some respect (e.g., culturally), for some social unit (e.g., a given person), in certain circumstances (e.g., in ordinary life), and in connection with a certain set of desiderata. In turn, desiderata themselves, as well as norms, or desirable patterns of behavior, are justi-

---

[44] Moore, *Principia ethica* (1903), pp. 77 *et passim*.

[45] For a criticism of the Fact/Value dichotomy, see Bunge, *Etica y ciencia* (1960).

[46] See Stern, "Significado de la fenomenología" (1944) and "Max Scheler, filósofo de la guerra total y del estado totalitario" (1945).

fiable both pragmatically (by their result) and theoretically: by their compatibility with laws of nature and society, and by their coherence with further desiderata and norms, some of which must, of course, be chosen as principles.[47]

Any such attempts to construct axiology and ethics with the help of analysis and science, of injecting into them nature, experience, and reason, and to cleanse them of mystery and dogma, are, of course, rejected by intuitionism.

A BALANCE SHEET

Some typical instances of philosophical intuitionism have been briefly discussed; let us now draw up a balance sheet.

(1) *The existence of the intuitions of intuitionists has not been demonstrated.* The intellectual intuition of Descartes, Leibniz, and Spinoza, is but a rapid inference; it is so quick that its mediate and learned character is usually not realized. As to Kant's pure intuition, it turned out to be a wrong mixture of reason and the consciousness of inner experience, and the products attributed to it by its inventor are inconsistent with both empirical and formal science as evolved after him.

The intuitions of Dilthey, Bergson, Husserl, Scheler, and other neo-Romantics—so closely related to Pythagorean "participation" and to Hermetic "sympathy"—have not even led to fruitful errors. They have given us nothing but the age-old and frustrated pretension of limiting the reach of experience and reason; they have not enabled us to attain a deeper understanding of history, or of life, or of a single essential property or essential law of any class of objects. How could they, if knowledge proper is conceptual and systematic? As Schlick wrote, intuition, if sensible, *gives* the object but does not *apprehend it conceptually,* so that the locution "intuitive knowledge" is a contradiction in terms.[48] Living and seeing may give some acquaintance with things ("know how") but never an un-

---

[47] For an attempt to provide a theoretical justification of value judgments and ethical norms, see Bunge, *Etica y ciencia* (1960), and "Ethics as a Science" (1961).
[48] Schlick, *Allgemeine Erkenntnislehre* (1925), pp. 76-7.

derstanding of things ("know that"). As to philosophical intuition, no wonder it is sterile if it does not exist.

In short, the many declarations about the power of intuition and the misery of reason have not been proven: they are typical samples of dogmatism.

(2) *Intuitionism is, from a logical point of view, a product of fundamentalism and infallibilism, both of which are untenable.* The quest for immovable foundations, for certain and self-evident truths, could not fail to suggest the existence of an extraordinary way of knowing, of a kind of natural revelation independent of both external experience and reason, since these are fallible and never establish absolute and eternal "foundations."

Unfortunately for intuitionism, the explicandum it tries to account for does not exist. There *are* no premises basic in an absolute sense; there are only *hypotheses* and *conventions* functioning as axioms, or postulates, in certain theoretical systems, i.e., *relative* to further propositions. And more often than not such axioms are not self-evident but result from a laborious work in search of the most perspicuous and economical arrangement of a body of knowledge.

Besides, "true science" is no longer defined as certain or indubitable knowledge (*episteme*) as opposed to uncertain and changeable opinion (*doxa*). Scientific knowledge is justifiable opinion, grounded opinion—but still opinion. If knowledge is secure, then it is not of fact but of form; and if it refers to reality, it is insecure, corrigible, perfectible.[49]

In other words, although there is certainty in much of formal science, there is almost none in empirical science. In questions of fact we must content ourselves with *practical certainty,* the kind we adopt when we do not attain or need a precision higher than a given value. The quest for definitive and tran-

---

[49] Recall Einstein's famous phrase, "As far as the laws of mathematics refer to reality, they are not certain; and as far as they are certain, they do not refer to reality." "Geometry and Experience" (1923), in Feigl and Brodbeck (Eds.), *Readings in Philosophy of Science,* p. 189.

quilizing certainty—which weak minds long for so intensely —has been replaced by the minimization of error, which is easier to discover than truth.[50] And one of the techniques for the minimization of error is the gradual *elimination,* or else the *elucidation* (or explication), of intuitive terms, not as a preliminary operation of purification but as an unending process of clarification (see *"Intuitive"* vs. *"Systematic,"* Chap. 3). Scientifically oriented minds find tranquilization in a grounded confidence in the progress of knowledge; in emergency cases, they may find it in certain pills.

Nobody, save the philosophically immature or naïve, believes nowadays in the possibility of an immediate and total grasp of truth. We all know that the adventure of cognition is risky and has no end, that it jumps from failure to failure, although the extent of every failure is usually smaller than that of the preceding one. We also know that there is neither an ultimate foundation nor a final certainty; that no intuition or experience is so secure that it can elude rational criticism; that the sciences have no ultimate foundation, but rather support and modify one another and are constantly changing their points of departure; and that in the field of knowledge there are no relations of absolute foundation but rather of relative logical antecedence. We are *revisionists* rather than fundamentalists, *fallibilists* rather than infallibilists. Even intuitionists are beginning to doubt the infallibility of intuition.[51]

(3) *Intuitionism is, from a psychological point of view, the product of a confusion.* By exaggerating a little we might say that intuitionism is the product of a linguistic equivocation: it comes about as a result of confusing *psychological* certainty, or self-evidence (which is said to characterize intuitions), with rigorous proof. The proof, once understood and synthetized,

---

[50] Popper, *The Logic of Scientific Discovery* (1935, 1959), and "On the Sources of Our Knowledge" (1959).

[51] Ewing, "Reason and Intuition" (1941), p. 25. While defending the existence and fundamental role of intuition, Professor Ewing grants that the intuitionist "must abandon the claim to certainty and infallibility which has been commonly advanced for intuition in the past."

gives us a feeling of self-evidence, to the extent that we often wonder how we could have failed to "see" it before. But the converse is not true: psychological certainty does not warrant logical validity or empirical validation.

In matters of daily life, we often confuse self-evidence, understood as maximal understanding and credibility, with truth. A mother rarely errs when, pointing to a child, she says "He is my son." Truth and self-evidence seem to be one and the same in the case of "direct" knowledge—to the extent that such a cognition exists. But in scientific matters, it usually happens that the deepest truths are "self-evident," if at all, only for those who have learned them laboriously, or applied them very often, or—even better—for those who have made or at least reconstructed them by themselves. Self-evidence is usually the mark of habit, hence a red light, since—dangerously enough—we do not tend to question or analyze what we are used to.

(4) *Intuitionism is a variety of dogmatism and leads to authoritarianism.* Since not everyone can grasp the basic truths and the essences, the alleged proprietor of the ability of suprarational intuition must be a person whose word ought to be revered. His intuitions are infallible and consequently indisputable.

Another, equally possible, consequence does not seem to have been extracted, namely, intuitionist anarchy, grounded on the following argument: if a given intuition is as good as any other, it is not corrigible by any other intuition; hence every knowledge is personal or private, whence a plurality of theories and even of world views results; and there is no possibility of choice among them, because they are equally valuable even though they are mutually inconsistent. In either case, with collective as well as with individual authoritarianism, dogmatism is asserted and objective truth is denied. In either case the possibility of the collective enterprise of gaining and improving cognition is absent.

It may rightly be argued that radical empiricism, e.g.,

sensism, and classical, aprioristic rationalism, are equally dogmatic and authoritarian in that they establish the existence of altogether reliable and incorrigible "ultimate sources" of knowledge. But at least sensible experience and reason *exist*, even if they are not found isolated from each other in the higher animals. But what could we say of a nonexistent faculty, an intuition which is neither sensible nor rational, and which is deemed capable of attaining the unattainable: secure foundations?

(5) *Intuitionism leads to irrationalism.* The existence and excellence of an activity independent of and higher than reason is first asserted, and, finally, reason is reviled. This degeneration of intuitionism into irrationalism, anti-intellectualism, and even sheer charlatanism, reached its highest peak in the Third Reich after a long period of preparation, in which intuitionists of all shades and all European nations, and even their cultural colonies, took part *nolens volens*. Nazi Germany exalted blood, instinct, "sympathetic understanding," or empathy, the vision of essences and the intuition of values and norms. As a compensation, it denigrated logic, criticism, the rational processing of experience, the theoretical transcending and explanation of experience, the slow, zigzagging and self-corrective search for truth.

The mention of the political role of intuitionism is not an *ad hominem* argument. Not only was intuitionism, alongside other forms of occultism and obscurantism, made official by Nazism, but it was also made part of its ideology and was consistent with its goal of barbarization and deculturation. Nazism itself was prepared, in the ideological sphere, by many a philosopher and "spirit scientist" (*Geisteswissenschaftler*) who exalted instinct and intuition over reason, the perception of wholeness over analysis, direct cognition over inferred knowledge (which is peculiar to science), self-evidence over proof.[52]

---

[52] See Kolnai, *The War Against the West* (1938), a superb exposition of Nazi ideology and its philosophical antecedents.

There was nothing accidental in this: a people brutalized by the dogma of antireason may more easily be induced to commit irrational acts than a people put on guard by criticism. Philosophical intuitionism thus ended by becoming a philosophy of the perverse for irrationals.

2

MATHEMATICAL
INTUITIONISM

SOURCES

Mathematical and philosophical roots

Sensible intuition and geometrical intuition, or the capacity for spatial representation or visual imagination, have very few defenders in mathematics nowadays, because it has been shown once and for all that they are as deceptive logically as they are fertile heuristically and didactically. Therefore, what is usually called mathematical intuitionism does not rely on sensible intuition.

An early example of the limitations of geometrical intuition was the invention of non-Euclidean geometries. A later example was the proof of the existence of an infinity of fractions between any two given fractions, however close they may be (e.g., between 999,999,999,999:1,000,000,000,000 and 1). Further instances were the continuous curves without a tangent, the curves filling a whole region of the plane; the single-face surfaces; transfinite numbers; and the 1:1 correspondence between the points in a line segment and those in a square, which runs counter to the "intuitive" notion of dimension.[1]

---

[1] Excellent examples of counterintuitive mathematical constructions are to be found in Rey Pastor, *Introducción a la matemática superior* (1916), and Hahn, "The Crisis of Intuition" (1933). It must be realized, however, that these counterexamples do not affect mathematical intuitionism, which proclaims the existence of a *pure* (non-sensible) intuition and forsakes geometrical intuition. Therefore, Hahn, *op. cit.*, and Schlick, in his *Allgemeine Erkenntnislehre* (1925), pp. 323 ff., because they only cite examples of the failure of *sensible* intuition in mathematics, do not prove their thesis—which nevertheless remains correct —that *pure* intuition, in the Kantian sense, is undependable.

It is now well understood that mathematical entities, relations, and operations, do not all originate in sensible intuition; it is realized that they are conceptual constructions that may altogether lack empirical correlates, even though some of them may serve as auxiliaries in theories about the world, such as physics. It is also recognized that self-evidence does not work as a criterion of truth, and that proofs cannot be shown by figures alone, because arguments are invisible. In particular, it is no longer required that axioms be "self-evident"; on the contrary, because they are almost always richer than the theorems they are designed to explain, axioms are often less "evident" than the theorems they give rise to, and are therefore apt to appear later than the theorems in the historical development of theories. Thus it is easier to obtain theorems on equilateral triangles than to establish general propositions about triangles.

After the failure of sensible and spatial (or geometrical) intuitions as reliable guides of mathematical construction, so-called *pure* intuition was to be tried. And since the Kantian pure intuition of space had become suspect even for some neo-Kantians, like Natorp and Cassirer, the pure intuition of time, or succession, had to be tried. This essay was made by the so-called mathematical intuitionism (or neointuitionism, as it prefers to call itself). Neointuitionism is far from being a puerility or a mere anti-intellectualist declamation. On the contrary, it constitutes an answer to legitimate and difficult problems that have preoccupied serious and profound thinkers like Henri Poincaré (1854-1912), Hermann Weyl (1885-1955), Brouwer (1881-   ), and Heyting (1898-   )—an answer that is certainly controvertible and in some respects even dangerous to the future of science.

Mathematical intuitionism is best understood if it is regarded as a current that originated among mathematicians (*a*) as a reaction against the exaggerations of logicism and formalism; (*b*) as an attempt to rescue mathematics from the shipwreck that, at the beginning of our century, the discovery of the paradoxes in set theory seemed to forecast; (c) as a minor product of Kantian philosophy (see *Kant's pure intuition*, Chap. 1).

Against logicists, who, like the medieval realists or Platonists,[2] speak of mathematical objects that exist independently of minds capable of constructing them effectively and of propositions that exist even in the absence of minds capable of proving them, mathematical intuitionists insist that only such entities exist—and this in the human mind, not in a Platonic realm of Ideas (logicism) or just on paper (formalism)—as are constructed, and only such statements are true which we have demonstrated in a direct or constructive way.

Against formalists (Kempe, Hilbert, and our contemporary, the mythical Bourbaki), who, like the medieval nominalists, assert that what we call mathematical objects are nothing but the marks we make on paper, intuitionists maintain that genuine mathematical objects are objects of thought, and those which are basic are intuitions (pure intuitions), whereas the derived ones are concepts.

As can be seen, mathematical intuitionism is closer to conceptualism—which would hold that "3" is a sign representing the concept of the number three and is not to be confused with the latter—than to philosophical intuitionism. Up to a certain point, mathematical intuitionism is backed by some mathematicians who react indignantly against the frivolous characterization of mathematics as a formal game (formalism) or as a mere application of logic (logicism). In this sense, mathematical intuitionism is a self-defense of the mathematical profession. Unfortunately, many of the weapons of the defenders are not much better than those of the attackers.

Brouwer and Kant

What does mathematical intuitionism, even in its orthodox formulation, expounded by Brouwer and Heyting, owe to

---

[2] The parallels between logicism and realism (or Platonism), formalism and nominalism (or signism), and intuitionism and conceptualism have been pointed out, among others, by Quine, *From a Logical Point of View* (1953), pp. 14-15.

philosophical intuitionism? Not much. It is only indebted to
Kant, who was as much a rationalist and an empiricist as he
was an intuitionist; and even what mathematical intuitionism
owes to Kant may be left aside without fear of seriously misun-
derstanding the theory—as has been recognized by Heyting,[3]
although Brouwer might not agree.

The debt of mathematical intuitionism to Kant boils down
to two ideas: (*a*) time—though not space according to neointui-
tionists—is an a priori form of intuition and is essentially involved in the number concept, which is generated by the operation of counting; (*b*) mathematical concepts are essentially constructible: they are neither mere marks (formalism) nor are they
apprehensible by their being ready-made (Platonic realism of
ideas); they are the work of human minds. The first assertion
is unmistakably Kantian, but the second will be granted by
many non-Kantian thinkers. Those mathematicians who are
sympathetic with mathematical intuitionism tend to accept the
second thesis while ignoring the first.

Moreover, the form in which the intuition of time takes part
in the construction of mathematics, according to Brouwer, is
anything but clearly intuitable, that is, immediate and self-
evident. In fact, according to this leading figure of mathematical intuitionism, the original intuition (*Urintuition*) of mathematics, which is "the fundamental phenomenon of mathematical thinking," is "the intuition of the bare two-oneness" (or
two-ity, another possible version of the Dutch *twee-eenigheid*);
and this intuition, being basic, cannot be further elucidated.[4]

Brouwer's intuition of the bare two-ity—which might be
the concept of sequence, or of iteration, or perhaps of linear
discrete order—creates not only the numbers 1 and 2 but also
all the remaining finite cardinals, "inasmuch as one of the elements of the two-oneness may be thought of as a new two-oneness, which process may be repeated indefinitely." Once the
natural numbers have been built—an intuitive and *pre*mathe-

[3] Heyting, "Intuitionism in Mathematics" (1958).
[4] Brouwer, "Intuitionism and Formalism" (1913).

matical operation—mathematics proper may begin. Since a large part of mathematics may be built on the arithmetic of natural numbers, which would be generated by the intuition of time, it follows that "the apriority of time does not only qualify the properties of arithmetic as synthetic a priori judgments, but it does the same for those of geometry," though certainly along an extended conceptual chain.

The sole "basal intuition" would, then, suffice to engender step by step and in a constructive or recursive form—not merely by means of "creative definitions" or by resorting to indirect proof—the whole of mathematics or, rather, the mathematics allowed by mathematical intuitionism, which is only a portion of "classical" (pre-intuitionist) mathematics.

The current mathematician, busy with enriching and clarifying his science, has never looked with sympathy upon the brutal amputation of mathematics required by intuitionism, nor upon the claim that mathematical work proceeds on the obscure *Urintuition* of the bare two-ity. On the other hand, he may sympathize with the constructivist program (see below, *The principle of constructivity*).

The ideas and the program of mathematical intuitionism were eventually made more precise[5] and, with this, the intuitionistic attitude came closer to that of its opponents. Nowadays most of the mathematicians interested in "foundation" questions and in the psychology of mathematical work seem to accept an assortment of theses taken from formalism, logicism, and intuitionism. Furthermore, to the extent that intuitionism takes an interest in the psychological aspect of mathematical work, it is compatible with both formalism and logicism, as is every pragmatic analysis with the corresponding syntactical analysis.

Mathematical intuitionism is definitely incompatible only with what may be termed the "ludic" conception of mathe-

[5] See Heyting, "Die intuitionistische Grundlegung der Mathematik" (1931), "La conception intuitionniste de la logique" (1956), and *Intuitionism: An Introduction* (1956).

matics—a ludicrous one, too—according to which the mathematical business is "a combinatorial game with the basic symbols," as von Neumann put it.[6]

MAIN THESES

It is worthwhile to examine and appraise the main theses of contemporary mathematical intuitionism. It will be seen that some are conceptualist, others pragmatist and others, finally, dynamicist; the admixture of philosophical intuitionism is scarce. Those theses are, in the writer's opinion, the following:

Status of logic and mathematics

(*1*) *The laws of logic are neither a priori nor eternal, contrary to what logicism maintains. They are hypotheses that man formulated when he studied the language by means of which he expressed his knowledge of finite sets of phenomena. As a consequence, the laws of logic should not be regarded as immutable regulative principles, but as corrigible hypotheses that may fail in connection with new kinds of objects, such as infinite sets.*

This conception of the nature and status of logic, far from being philosophically intuitionistic, might be shared by empiricists, pragmatists, materialists, and historicists. The history of logical and mathematical paradoxes should warn us that this thesis is worth being pondered over. There is no warrant against the possibility that further radical changes in formal logic will be required in the future in order to improve its adaptation to the actual inferential mechanisms and to new, unforeseeable kinds of entities and operations. Moreover, a number of mathematicians and logicians—it suffices to recall Lewis, Gentzen, Carnap, Reichenbach, and Popper—have proposed new formalizations of the relations of implication and deducibility. Many are beginning to doubt that ordinary logic

[6] von Neumann, "Die formalistische Grundlegung der Mathematik" (1931).

is an adequate reconstruction of the syntax of ordinary language or even of scientific language.

Mathematical intuitionists seem to be right in regarding the whole of logic as subject to possible ulterior revision. They are not right, on the other hand, when they hold that there are certain *mathematical* propositions—those which are declared to be intuitive—which are self-evident and consequently more secure than the logical ones. In contrast to the "queer" logics that are invented for purposes other than the reconstruction of ordinary inferential patterns, ordinary logic is adapted to science. Science bases the greater or lesser certainty of its inferences (not of its premises, which remain forever doubtful) on the laws of logic. Or, perhaps better: the good inferential patterns are those which are both successful in science and consecrated by logic.

The relation existing between logic and other sciences is not of one-sided dependence but of mutual and progressive adjustment.[7] Here, as elsewhere, improvements in the tool lead to progress in the attainment of the goal, and failures to reach the goal are fed back into the handling of the tool, so as to correct it and thereby increase its efficiency. Or are we to forget that Aristotelian logic was born in intimate contact with cosmology and biology, and that modern logic was mainly the work of mathematicians and philosophers of mathematics?

Mathematical intuitionists should not be criticized for espousing a fallibilist philosophy of logic; they are to be blamed for insisting on an infallibilist philosophy of mathematics.

(2) *Mathematics is a product of the human mind. As such, mathematics is a pure discipline, i.e., independent of experience, although it can be applied to experience; furthermore, mathematics is autonomous, i.e. independent of the other*

---

[7] The validity of logic rests upon its good performance in mathematics and in the factual sciences, and the validity of mathematics consists in its abidance by the laws of logic. This is not a vicious circle but a process of successive approximations, as was pointed out by Bôcher, "The Fundamental Conceptions and Methods of Mathematics" (1905). See also Goodman, *Fact, Fiction, & Forecast* (1954).

sciences and, particularly, autonomous with regard to logic.
This thesis is not typically intuitionistic in a philosophical
sense. In part it may be maintained by any mathematician who
believes in the possibility of building the whole of mathematics
on the basis of set theory.

What few philosophers would be prepared to admit is the
Kantian thesis that mathematics is entirely prior to and independent of logic, especially since logical concepts (such as "all,"
"some," "and," "not," "if . . . then—") are woven in the
very fabric of mathematics. Any mathematician would confirm
that he explicitly employs logical laws, such as those of identity,
contradiction, and detachment. But, of course, his work does
not consist in a purely logical computation: after all somebody
has to "see" the problem, invent the adequate premisses, suspect the relevant relations, and establish bridges among different
territories of mathematics. Moreover, it has been shown that
intuitionist mathematics, far from being prior to logic, is based
on intuitionist logic.[8]

David Hilbert (1862-1943), the leading figure of the formalist
camp, would not have quarreled with the above intuitionist
thesis, since he wrote that mathematics, just as any other science, cannot be founded on logic alone but requires the assumption of prelogical objects[9]; but such prelogical objects
are, for formalism, marks, i.e., physical objects, and not concepts.

Hilbert, too, regarded logic as an application of mathematics.
Intuitionism and formalism agree, then, with regard to the
psychological (and even logical!) priority of mathematics over
logic. In this sense, both constitute an inverted logicism, and to
this extent both are highly controvertible. To say with Kant,
Brouwer, and Hilbert that mathematical *research* is quite independent of logic is to make an assertion relevant to the *psychology* of mathematics. The assertion would be true if construed in this way: mathematicians are not usually aware that

[8] Beth, "Semantic Construction of Intuitionist Logic" (1956).
[9] Hilbert, "Über das Unendliche" (1925).

they use logic. Likewise, Monsieur Jourdain, Molière's character, did not know that he had been talking prose all his life. A good mathematician may be quite ignorant of logic, just as a good novelist may ignore grammar. This does not prove that their discourses are deprived of a formal skeleton, but only that they do not care for the sort of conceptual X rays that would enable the hidden structure to be rendered visible.

As to the pure or a priori nature of mathematics, this thesis is now granted by the vast majority of metascientists, with the exception of most materialists and pragmatists. This has been the case especially since it was realized that such an apriority is not at variance with the conception of mathematics as a part of culture and as a tool for action, and that it is compatible with the naturalistic view of mind as a function of the central nervous system.

But consistency would seem to require abandoning the Kantian belief—shared by Brouwer, though not by Heyting[10]—that mathematics is *applicable* to experience. One should admit, on the other hand, that mathematics does not apply either to reality or to experience, but to some of the *theories* (physical, biological, social, etc.) that refer to reality; in other words, mathematics may occur as a formal tool in theories that provide a schematic and tentative picture of objects assumed to be real.

The above remark about the *indirect* road leading from mathematics to the real, via factual theory and experience, may put an end to an old objection that has been raised and repeated *ad nauseam* against both logicism and formalism, namely, that they do not account for "the application of mathematics to experience." How could they account for such a thing if mathematics is *never* applied to facts—notwithstanding the misnomer "applied mathematics," which can still be found in books and university curricula? Mathematics is applicable only

---

[10] Heyting, *Intuitionism: An Introduction* (1956), p. 89: "The characteristic of mathematical thought is, that it does not convey truth about the external world, but is only concerned with mental constructions." On the other hand, Brouwer regards mathematical laws as laws of nature; see his "Intuitionism and Formalism" (1913).

to certain *ideas* about facts, and such ideas are material or factual (e.g., physical), not formal, in the sense that they have an objective or empirical referent.

(3) Mathematical signs are not void but designate mathematical objects, and the latter are, in turn, thought objects (concepts and judgments) which somehow reflect phenomena. In other words, mathematical objects, far from being self-existent (as the logicist claims), constitute "fields of constructive possibilities," and mathematical laws are a priori laws of nature.

These statements are not typically intuitionistic either, in the philosophical sense of "intuitionism." The former is conceptualist, whereas the claim that there are synthetic a priori judgments is epistemologically idealist and, more precisely, Kantian. That mathematics *in the making* is a mental activity will be denied only by the most extreme behaviorists and phenomenalists, who do not grant the existence of the mind, but who, by way of compensation, are rarely interested in mathematics.

What nonintuitionists maintain is that mental activities—or, if preferred, the activities of the brain cortex—should not be regarded from a psychological point of view only, that is, as a process, but from other points of view as well. The structure of the products of such activity is particularly worthy of examination. Why should the logician be deprived of the pleasure of analyzing these products, if the chemist is not denied the right to analyze the ashes left by fire?

As to the affirmation that mathematical laws are at the same time laws of nature, curiously enough it is shared by traditional empiricists, materialists, and objective idealists. It does not resist the simplest semantic, or even historical, analysis. Would experience be needed for disclosing the patterns of reality if that contention were true? And why do most scientific hypotheses that are clad in a correct mathematical form eventually turn out to be false? One and the same mathematical skeleton may be endowed with a plurality of meanings, but then it ceases to be purely mathematical; and some of the interpreted mathematical structures will be true whereas others will be false.[11]

The intuitionist thesis of mathematical intuitionism

(4) *Since mathematics is not derived from either logic or experience, it must originate in a special intuition that presents us the basic concepts and inferences of mathematics as immediately clear and secure. "A mathematical construction ought to be so immediate to the mind and its results so clear that it needs no foundation whatsoever."* [12] *We should consequently choose as basic notions the most immediate ones, such as those of natural number and existence.*

This is, in the writer's opinion, *the* unequivocally intuitionist thesis of mathematical intuitionism. And it is a very vulnerable contention. In fact, although the digits are psychologically clear, this is not the case with the *infinite* sequence of natural numbers, a relatively late invention which most people find difficult to grasp.

As an eminent Bourbakian points out, the assignment of a privileged role to natural numbers is based upon

a psychological confusion between the particularly clear and immediate intuition we have of the properties of small numbers and the extension of these properties to *all* integers, an extension which, in my opinion, derives from purely arbitrary axioms. We have not, and without any doubt we cannot have the least intuition (in the classical sense of this word) of large numbers such as $100^{100^{100}}$; to say that the definition of $n + 1$ for such a number n is intuitively clear and that the property $n + 1 > n$ is a self-evident truth, has always seemed to me to be nonsense. And if it is accepted it is difficult to see what could prevent us from returning to the classical conception of the axioms of Euclidean geometry, which were also regarded as self-

[11] See Carnap, *Foundations of Logic and Mathematics* (1939).
[12] Heyting, *Intuitionism: An Introduction* (1956), p. 6.

evident by a similar "extrapolation"; it is well known, however, that this is an untenable attitude.[13]

As to the notion of existence, another immediately clear concept according to intuitionism, it is well known that it raises a number of difficulties in logic, mathematics, and epistemology. We still dispute whether existence is a property or merely a quantifier, or whether one should distinguish and accept various meanings of "existence" (possible and actual, formal and material, and so on).

Questions of existence are not always easy to answer. Where and how do centaurs and solutions of differential equations exist? Do transfinite numbers exist in the same sense as ordinary numbers? Does the millionth partial sum of a power series exist even though nobody has computed it effectively? Did the property of π of being transcendental (non-algebraic) exist before it was demonstrated? Most mathematicians would give affirmative answers to these mathematical questions, which intuitionists answer in the negative. Why, then, do intuitionists claim that formal existence, which is actually an elusive concept, is clear and basic and in no need of analysis?

On the other hand, intuitionists are not alone when they affirm that mathematics is grounded on premathematical intuition. This same thesis was expounded by Hilbert from about 1921 on. Hilbert acknowledged not only the existence of extralogical objects that are given in perception before being thought, but also the existence of intuitive and reliable procedures, such as the recognition of the first time a sign appears in a succession of marks, and even the basic logical inference pattern (the *modus ponens*). This is why it has been pointed out that, although the first step in Hilbert's work was the elimination of intuition, the second step led to its rehabilitation.[14]

---

[13] Dieudonné, "L'axiomatique dans les mathématiques modernes" (1951), p. 51.

[14] Baldus, *Formalismus und Intuitionismus in der Mathematik* (1924), pp. 31-32. Hilbert's views can be seen in his *Grundlagen der Geometrie*, Appendices to later editions.

However, the qualification must be made that Hilbert's is not a mystical *pure* intuition, independent of ordinary experience. It is the old *sensuous* intuition, or sense perception, as applied specifically to the apprehension and recognition of marks on the paper or on the blackboard and to the imagining of geometrical correlates of analytical entities. Did not Hilbert maintain that the objects of mathematics are the concrete signs themselves, and that it is possible to attain mathematical truth "in a purely intuitive and finite way"? [15] And did he not write a textbook of *Intuitive Geometry* full of beautiful and suggestive drawings designed to produce understanding with the help of sight? [16] Were these facts more widely known, mathematical formalism would not be confused with *abstractism*, or the cult of ideal forms. The "formalism" of Hilbert and Bourbaki is, like the nominalism of the Middle Ages, the early Quine, and Lorenzen, a variety of "vulgar" materialism.

Yet when Hilbert proclaims, *"Am Anfang ist das Zeichen"* ("In the beginning is the sign"), and when he states his confidence in the sensible operations (seeing and writing) with physical marks (symbols), enabling us to *secure* a proposition, he exhibits the same fundamentalist and infallibilist tendency that originates philosophical and mathematical intuitionism. Furthermore, he repeatedly asserted that his aim was to attain "the definitive security (*Sicherheit*) of mathematical methods." [17]

A critical and at the same time tolerant metascientist (whose existence would be hard to prove) would deny the existence of mathematical entities that are fundamental in an *absolute* sense. But he would admit, on the other hand, a multiplicity of essays in foundations, with the sole restriction that they be self-consistent and not bring about mutilations of mathematics. What he would definitely disavow is the existence of concepts *intrinsically* self-evident or clear. He would know that self-

[15] Hilbert, "Über das Unendliche" (1925).
[16] Hilbert and Cohn-Vossen, *Anschauliche Geometrie* (1932).
[17] Hilbert, reference 15.

evidence is a psychological relation, not a logical property; and he would point out further that the degree of self-evidence depends to a large extent upon each person's experience or background.[18]

What ground is there for believing that certain concepts and propositions are in *all* respects (logically, psychologically, historically, etc.) more fundamental than others? What ground is there for thinking that there are ultimate foundations in any science, or that definitive systems may be built? What guarantees that the set concept, at present regarded as the basic concept of mathematics, will not be replaced by some other notion? There is no more a thousand-year kingdom in mathematics than there is in politics.

The principle of constructivity

(5) *The sole admissible technique of demonstration of existence theorems is effective construction, because it permits us to "see" what it is all about. On the other hand, the demonstration that the assumption contradicting the one that is to be proved leads to a contradiction, i.e., the technique of indirect demonstration, does nothing but point to a possibility of existence or of truth, without warranting it. Now explicit or effective construction is possible, by definition, only with finitist procedures, that is, by means of a finite number of signs and operations, such as is the case with the computation of the square of a number, or with the application of the principle of mathematical (complete) induction. Hence, all propositions involving infinite classes regarded as totalities must be excluded from mathematics. Similarly, expressions such as "for any class," "the class of all primes," and "the class of all classes," as well as the theorems that are demonstrated in an essentially indirect way (as are most theorems in Cantor's theory of sets) must be eliminated or reconstructed.*

This is the "constructivist" rule of intuitionist mathematics.

---

[18] Those who deal with abstract objects acquire an "intuition" about them. See Dieudonné, *loc. cit.*

It had been anticipated by Kronecker, a minor figure, and by Poincaré, a major one, and it is the more interesting for mathematicians because it has practical consequences of long range or, better, of a tremendous reducing power. Before analyzing it, we should see how it works.

The intuitionist will not grant the existence of a number just because the sequence of the operations necessary for constructing it is laid down; he wants actuality, not mere possibility. Thus he will not believe that the number (the concept) corresponding to the sign "1000^{1000}" exists, nor will he admit a priori the truth of the alternative: "The number 1000^{1000} can be decomposed or cannot be decomposed into the sum of two prime numbers." He will wait until the actual decomposition has been performed, or until it has been proven impossible. In general, for the mathematical intuitionist the statement: "There exists at least one x such that x has the property P" means that a mathematical object a satisfying the condition $P(a)$ has been constructed.[19]

Just as the naïve realist says, "Seeing is believing" and the operationalist holds that "To be is to be measured," the intuitionist seems to say, "Effectively computing is believing" and "To exist is to be constructed." And once the number (or the function) has been computed, he may stubbornly maintain— as have extreme empiricists—that it still is a nonsignificant sign. It is either not an intuitively apprenhensible sign, or it does not correspond to any actual experience—although physicists do not mind using numbers as large as 10^{80} or as small as 10^{-40}.

Euclid's indirect proof of the existence of an infinity of prime numbers will elicit a similar reaction from the intuitionist. Since the proof does not provide a function $f(n)$ for the effective computation of the n-th prime (given any integer n), such an infinity does not exist for him. And if we wished to prove Goldbach's conjecture, that every even number equals

---

[19] Heyting, "Some Remarks on Intuitionism," in Heyting (Ed.), *Constructivity in Mathematics* (1959), p. 70.

the sum of two primes, by saying that the assumption that there exists an even number which does *not* satisfy it leads to a contradiction with accepted propositions, the intuitionist would then ask us to produce a direct proof or to exhibit a counter-example by computing *effectively* an even number that does not satisfy Goldbach's conjecture. The same will happen with Cantor's proof, by the so-called diagonal procedure, that the continuum is not denumerable. Since the proof is indirect, it will have no appeal to the intuitionist, who may reject it for the same reason as the operationalist.[20]

With regard to the existential statements of mathematics, the intuitionist operates in a way similar to the natural scientist. Suppose a physicist wants to prove the proposition: "There are elements with an atomic number larger than 102(Nobelium)." He will try to produce a sample of a transnobelian. He will not remain content with saying that, if transnobelians *did* exist, nuclear theory *would* lead to an absurd proposition, because the theory is known to contain absurd propositions. But the physicist will not, therefore, disdain every preliminary theoretical research into the *possibility* of the existence of such an element, and such a possibility will consist in the compatibility of the assumption with the known laws of nature. On the contrary, he will try to estimate, for instance, the ratio between the repulsive force of protons and the attractive specific forces maintaining the cohesion of the hypothetical 103 nucleus. And this will enable him to predict that, if the element does exist, then it will probably be highly unstable owing to the predominance of repulsive over attractive forces; from instability he will conclude that the probable element will be short-lived, and from this he will conclude the need for very delicate methods of detection. His conclusion, "Transnobelians probably exist," will therefore have some value—a heuristic value—although the information content of that proposition will certainly be lower than that of "Eureka! I have just produced a sample of a transnobelian!"

[20] Bridgman, *Reflections of a Physicist* (1955), pp. 101 ff.

The mathematical intuitionist is right when he insists that the existence proof says less, i.e., provides us with less information, than the effective construction whereby the object whose existence has been secured is actually exhibited. Consider the distance between the fundamental theorem of algebra, which warrants the *existence* of n roots of every algebraic equation of the n-th degree, and the poor algorithms available for the effective computation of these roots for $n > 4$. An existence statement which does not enable us to identify precisely that which is asserted to exist is—in the words of Weyl—like a document describing minutely a treasure without saying where it is.[21]

On the other hand, the nonintuitionist is justified in prizing such a document. Not all the propositions need have a maximal content. And existence theorems, even though they do not enable us to individualize those objects whose existence they secure, do enable us to make inferences that may eventually lead to effective, even if only approximate, computation. Thus, for instance, we know that an algebraic equation of the 10th degree has 10 roots, even though we have no general algorithm for building them. And the existence statement is needed if we are to undertake the approximate computation of these solutions, just as a description of the treasure is needed if we are to embark on an exploration to unearth it. In general, the inference to singular propositions requires not only universal premises but also existential and/or singular propositions.

Now constructivism is not the monopoly of mathematical intuitionism. Thus the Polish school of constructivist mathematics allows all methods of proof, and its constructivism consists in the fact that it considers only those objects for which there are effective methods of exact or approximate computation.[22] This is why Heyting distinguishes, within the genus of constructivist mathematics, *theories of the constructible* (e.g.,

[21] Weyl, *Philosophy of Mathematics and Natural Science* (1926, 1949), pp. 50-51.

[22] See Andrzej Grzegorczyk, "Some Approaches to Constructive Analysis," in Heyting (Ed.), *Constructivity in Mathematics* (1959), p. 43.

those of the Polish constructivists) and *constructive theories.*
The latter do not remain satisfied with the *possibility* of construction but require the effective construction of the mathematical objects dealt with.[23]

One cannot refrain from asking whether in either case there is a clear historical perspective about the *relative* character of constructivity. The Greeks took it for granted that any acceptable solution to a geometrical problem should be attained with the exclusive use of ruler and compass; the invention of analytic geometry by Descartes made this requirement obsolete. The very notion of constructivity has changed. What reason is there to expect that it will not change again, and that it will remain a desideratum?

In any case, the constructivist injunction should not be characterized as intuitionist from a philosophical point of view. (Heyting calls the constructivist injunction the "principle of positivity" and states it in the form: "Every mathematical or logical statement [admitted by intuitionism!] expresses the result of a construction." [24]) It is, rather, a *pragmatist* prescription, although it is usually assigned a Kantian origin.[25]

It is true that Kant maintained that mathematics is the rational knowledge obtained from the "construction of concepts." But what Kant meant by "construction" was not, for instance, the formation of an algorithm for the effective computation or construction of an expression like $100^{100^{100}}$, but rather the exhibition of the *pure intuition* corresponding to the concept in question.[26] For Kant, "to build a concept means to give its corresponding a priori intuition"—which, if possible, would be a psychological operation—whereas, for mathematical intuitionism, the construction may be entirely logical, to the point that it may consist in the deduction of a contradiction. The *ultimate foundation* of all mathematical concepts, which for

[23] Heyting, reference 19 above.
[24] Heyting, "La conception intuitionniste de la logique" (1956), p. 223.
[25] See Black, *The Nature of Mathematics* (1933), p. 190.
[26] Kant, *Kritik der reinen Vernunft*, pp. 741 ff.

Kant and Brouwer alike must be intuitive, is quite another matter. Unlike Kant, the mathematical intuitionist will require that only the *basic* ideas be intuitive.

The thesis of constructivism in its strict, intuitionist form, is at bottom a *semantic thesis of an operationalist kind*. It tells us, indeed: (a) "There is at least one x such that x has the property P," means that at least one x has been shown to have the property P. (b) "All x are P" means that given any particular x, we may prove (even better, we have proved) by direct methods that this x is a P.

The constructivist rule, then, is clearly pragmatist (operationalist) rather than intuitionist, since it amounts to the semantic thesis: "The meaning of an expression is the set of operations enabling us to construct it or to verify it"—a thesis defended by Wittgenstein (1889-51), the Vienna Circle (ca. 1925-1936), and Bridgman, no less than by Weyl.

In point of fact, as early as 1926 and completely independent of logical empiricism and operationalism, Weyl wrote, "Whenever the *possibility* of a construction is being asserted, we have no meaningful proposition; only by virtue of an effective construction, an executed proof, does an existential statement [such as "There exists an even number"] acquire meaning." [27] (Remember that, strictly speaking, an existential statement is an infinite logical sum—an impossible *operation*.) When Brouwer holds that a theorem does not express a truth (since truth does not exist apart from our knowledge) but the success of a systematic construction, is he not taking a definite pragmatist stand, even though this kinship has not been pointed out? And when Heyting maintains that "a mathematical proposition expresses a given expectation," [28] is he not adopting *avant la lettre* a thesis of Morris' behaviorist semiotics?

In fighting Platonism, intuitionists, formalists, nominalists, and operationalists will deprive mathematics of nonconstructible entities which the bulk of mathematicians cherish. By so

[27] Weyl, *Philosophy of Mathematics and Natural Science* (1926, 1949), p. 51.
[28] Heyting, "Die intuitionistische Grundlegung der Mathematik" (1931), p. 113.

doing they may chase away some ghosts, but at the same time they tear down many useful and beautiful structures. In science, as in life, progress involves risk. The slogan "Safety first," adopted by infallibilism, is incompatible with the desideratum of fruitfulness. Nothing is safer than the grave.

(6) *Only constructive or potential infinity exists. Actual or complete infinity, the infinite collection regarded as given or laid down, which Cantor's set theory studies, is an illusion: it does not exist, since it is not constructible.*

In the conception of infinity lies another major technical difference between intuitionist mathematics and the usual approach. It must not be forgotten (see *Mathematical and philosophical roots*) that mathematical intuitionism was partly born as an effort to free mathematics and logic from the paradoxes that had been discovered in the theory of infinity at the beginning of our century.

But the opposition to actual infinity is not, of course, peculiar to mathematical intuitionism. It was shared by dynamicists like Hegel and by all empiricists, including Aristotle— whose epistemology was basically empiricist—and Locke (1632-1704), for whom actual infinity, in contradistinction to potential infinity, was "inconceivable" and consequently a *flatus vocis* rather than a concept. Hilbert, too, regarded actual infinity as "something merely apparent," whether in the realm of experience or in mathematics. And the engineers, who are always content with approximations, should welcome finitist mathematics almost as much as those local statesmen who ruled that the value of π is 3.1.

The historian of science knows that the evolution of knowledge has been, to some extent, a sequence of creations initially regarded as "inconceivable," "absurd," or even "crazy." Every new deep theory, whether true or false, is apt to appear mad. The epistemologist will say that "conceivable," "sound," and related terms are psychological categories and not marks of existence or signs of truth, whether in mathematics or elsewhere. And the mathematician will refuse to cut off, in the name of intuition and constructivity, that monument of human reason and boldness called set theory and which has become a basis— perhaps neither definitive nor the sole possible one—of most contemporary mathematics.

Rather, the mathematician will assume an even more con-structive attitude than the champions of constructivism: he will try to cleanse the theory of actual infinity instead of eliminat-ing it. In this way he will continue the tradition of Weier-strass, who replaced the "infinitely small" and "infinitely large" of analysis by relations among finite quantities.

The excluded middle

(7) *The law of the excluded middle must be suspended, not eliminated. It is neither a self-evident nor a demonstrated proposition, and as a methodological auxiliary it is inconsistent with the principle of constructivity or positivity* (see The prin-ciple of constructivity), *since a proposition is true only if it has been constructively demonstrated; otherwise it may not only be false but also for the time being undecided or even essen-tially undecidable.*

For the intuitionist, logic is not a formal calculus but a *methodology,* a "logic of knowledge" (Heyting) dealing with the organization and transformation of our inferences. And in a system of logic conceived in this way there cannot be propo-sitions true or false *per se,* apart from the process of their vali-dation.

According to this there is no difference between truth and knowledge of the truth, so that only intuited or demonstrated propositions can be treated as true. Why care for propositions that have neither been intuited nor been shown to be either true or false, if they do not *exist?* Unverified propositions have as little place in this logic as meaningless noises. Thus, for in-stance, it makes no sense for the intuitionist to predicate any-thing about the millionth decimal figure of π. Since it does not *exist* in the intuitionist sense—we have not computed it effec-tively—we cannot say that it *is* either even *or* odd, prime *or* composite. Likewise, the atheist abstains from saying that God *is* either omniscient or *is* not omniscient; this alternative will be entirely beyond his interest. The suspension of the third excluded "principle" is seen to be consistent with the rule of constructivity.

From such an identification of truth with either intuition or demonstration it follows that, in the absence of an effective demonstration of p and of not-p, we cannot assert that there are only two possibilities, namely, p and not-p (law of the excluded middle); we cannot even state that this disjunction is false. Notice that, contrary to a widespread misconception, in intuitionistic logic the law of the excluded middle is not rejected: it is shown, with all rigor, that "it is absurd that the law of the excluded middle be absurd."

Intuitionist logic does not admit a third *truth value*, as is often believed, but rather a third *category of propositions* besides the true and the false ones, namely, those about which it makes no sense to say that they are true or that they are false. Such indeterminate statements may eventually be shown to be either true, or false, or essentially undecidable with the help of a prescribed set of techniques.

The statement: "The millionth decimal figure of π is even" is as meaningless for the intuitionist as is its contradictory statement. On the other hand, for the nonintuitionist a definition of π by means of an infinite series, such as

$$\pi = 4 \left(\frac{1}{1} - \frac{1}{3} + \frac{1}{5} - \cdots \right),$$

creates the totality of its decimal figures even though we have not effected the sum up to the last term necessary to *know* whether its millionth decimal figure is even or odd. The current mathematician, then, distinguishes truth from *knowledge* of the truth when he takes it for granted that the phrase: "The millionth decimal figure of π is even" is either true or false.

Take another example: consider a number such as e^π, or the

Euler-Mascheroni constant C,[29] of neither of which we know

$$C =_{df} \lim_{n \to \infty} (1 + \frac{1}{2} + \frac{1}{3} + \cdots + \frac{1}{n} - \log n) = 0.57721566 \cdots$$

whether it is algebraic (a solution of some algebraic equation with integral coefficients) or transcendental (non-algebraic). The mathematician who accepts ordinary logic will say, for instance, "C is algebraic or transcendental," thereby accepting the law of the excluded middle. The intuitionist, on the other hand, will claim "C will be algebraic, or will be transcendental, once it has been demonstrated that it is the one or the other, and on condition that the proof be carried out with constructive methods. For the time being C is neither algebraic nor transcendental."

Notice that this is not hairsplitting but a genuine and deep problem involving the question of the nature of ideal (e.g., mathematical) entities, the theory of truth, the role time may play in it, and the status of logic. *If* logic is conceived in a purely methodological or epistemological sense—as intuitionists, along with materialists and pragmatists, conceive—and *if* the redefinition of "true proposition" as "intuited or demonstrated proposition" is adopted, then intuitionists are right in suspending the law of the excluded middle with regard to theorems (but not so with regard to axioms, since these are not demonstrable and may not be "intuitive" in the system in which they occur).

But what is the reason for dismissing formal logic in the name of methodology? What is the justification for identifying propositions of the form "A is B" with those of the form "We know (or we may prove) that A is B"? In other words, why should we erase the difference between semantics and pragmatics, between *truth and knowledge of truth*? [30] These distinctions are needed

---

[29] The Euler-Mascheroni constant may be defined in various ways; one of them is the following:

[30] For a defense of the distinction between truth and knowledge of the truth, see Baylis, "Are Some Propositions Neither True Nor False?" (1936).

to account for the daily work of mathematicians and scientists. Suppose a mathematician sets himself the task of evaluating the sum of an infinite series. He first makes sure that such a sum *exists:* even before *knowing* a particular truth he proves that it exists. To this end he applies certain decision procedures, the convergence criteria. (The fact that much too often such criteria do not allow a definite decision is another matter.) By so doing, the mathematician assigns a truth value to the proposition: "The given series has a finite sum S." He next proceeds to compute S. Suppose he does not succeed in computing it exactly; he will then try to obtain a certain approximate value S_n, e.g., by adding n terms. If he then says, "The sum of the series is S_n," he utters a partial truth. The amount of his error will be the excess of S over S_n, i.e., $S - S_n$, an indeterminate number measuring the "distance" between the partial but perfectible truth, "The sum of the series is S_n," and the total but unknown truth, i.e., the statement expressing the exact value S. It makes sense for him to say that by taking a larger number of terms he will get a better approximation to the total truth, even granting that such a total truth is unattainable. Similar situations arise in the whole of "applied" mathematics. In all such cases the mathematician believes that there *is* a true proposition, namely, about an exact value which he cannot attain. At least he will admit that such a true statement is *possible* even though he is not able to utter it. He thereby acknowledges, as it were, a *potential truth* which he can know only approximately.

Even if we do not *know* that A is B, even if we are unable to know that it is possible to demonstrate that A is B (or that A is not B), we are bound to *try the hypothesis* "A is B," treating it *as if* it were true (or false). This assumption is a presupposition of the hypothetico-deductive method reigning in science. The fertility and the charm of scientific investigation lies precisely in the ceaseless guessing of hypotheses and in the investigation of their logical consequences (see *Creative imagination,* Chap. 3). What would remain of science if it were forbidden to utter sentences of the form: "Suppose that A is B" one thousand times a day? Any attempt to exclude the tentative from science is incompatible with the spirit of scientific research and with the very conception of theories as hypothetico-deductive systems. Formal logic permits exploration of the consequences of well-formed hypotheses, however wild they may look. Such an exploration is what ultimately enables us to know anything, even though the knowledge that is attained may not be definitive. It is dangerous to curtail a discipline, in this case the strictly two-valued logic, in the name of the infallibilist tenet. For this and nothing else pushes intuitionists to require the *replacement* of formal logic by a logic of knowledge founded on the theory of knowledge (as if the latter might be conceived apart from logic). In fact, according to Heyting, "in the applications of logic, what we know and the conclusions that we may draw from what we know are always concerned." [31]

But is not what we *hypothesize* or assume more both in bulk and in importance than what we *know* with certainty? In order to pursue any scientific research whatsoever, it is indispensable that we treat all propositions making sense in a given context *as if* they were capable of neatly taking the values T or F. Yet, strictly speaking, we presume that—at least in connection with factual science—we can only reach approximate truths, so that in the end all that we "know" may turn out to be altogether false.

It should be frankly recognized that scientists tacitly adopt a *dualistic* theory of truth, whereby one and the same factual proposition is assigned a degree of adequacy (factual truth) lying between extreme falsity and extreme truth, and a logical truth value (F or T), depending upon whether the proposition is regarded as accurately descriptive of reality or as a premiss or a conclusion in logical inference. Such a dualistic theory of truth should retain ordinary logic—as the scientists do—but should elucidate the notion of partial truth.[32]

Scientific research is exploratory, and ordinary logic leaves

---

[31] Heyting, "La conception intuitionniste de la logique" (1956), p. 228.
[32] See Bunge, "A Mathematical Theory of Partial Truth" (forthcoming).

exploration more freedom than intuitionist logic does. And, after all, freedom of exploration is as vital for mathematicians as it is for geographers. Yet it must be admitted that the Kantian and Brouwerian proposal to regard the truth of mathematical propositions as a result of mental operations and not as a property they do or do not possess even in the absence of every verification procedure, is more reasonable and down to earth than the Plantonist attitude adopted by logicism and by most mathematicians. But we are not forced to choose between the Kantian solution, which at bottom is somewhat empiricist, and the logicist proposal, which is idealist. They do not exhaust all the possibilities.

In fact, every proposition may be regarded from various complementary points of view, among which the logical, the epistemological, and the psychological ones are particularly interesting. If we write "p," we limit ourselves to the former; but if we write "Asserted p," or "Demonstrated p," or "Rejected p," we enter the *methodological* field. The assertion of a proposition says something about the truth value we assign to it, whether in final form or by way of trial (in order to be able to explore its consequences). If, finally, we write, "I think that p," or "I hold p to be likely," or "x holds that p," we go over to the field of the *psychology* of knowledge. Why should we restrict the study of propositions to their methodological or psychological aspects? If we seriously assert that mathematical objects must be considered *only* as thought objects, then we must conclude that mathematics is a branch of psychology, and we must admit abnormal mathematical theories as much as we admit pathological thinking.

In favor of mathematical intuitionism it must be said that the demonstration by Gödel, in 1931, that in every formal system there are *demonstrably undecidable* propositions, did not constitute a catastrophe for intuitionism as it did for formalism. This discovery forced the conclusion that the alternative "True p or false p" is untenable *within* every formal system, since there are true but undecidable propositions. In other words, these propositions are somehow recognized as true but cannot be shown to be true with means weaker than, or at most as powerful as those allowed by the system under consideration. Still it must always be borne in mind that undecidability, i.e., impossibility of *formal* derivation, is not an intrinsic but a contextual property. The question of decidability arises always in connection with the possibility of deciding, on the basis of given axioms and given *finitist* rules of inference, what the truth value of a proposition is. If either the axiom system or the rules of inference are widened, a decision may eventually be reached, so that, finally, the exclusive and exhaustive disjunction "true *p* or false *p*" is assertible.

Hilbert's optimistic thesis, "Every problem is solvable," has, therefore, not been shown to be false. We cannot assert with certainty that there are essentially or intrinsically unsolvable problems of decision, that is, problems of demonstration that resist being approached by *any* method, whether available or inventable. It still is more prudent and more profitable to say that there are *unsolved* problems, or formally *underived* theorems—but surely this is trivial. Interpreted in this way, Gödel's results reinforce neither intuitionism nor irrationalism.

The discovery of the existence of formally undecidable propositions restricts the field of the dichotomy True/False with regard to truth as recognized by rigorous (formal) means. But some propositions, e.g., those of elementary arithmetic, may be recognized as true in an informal or semirigorous way, even though they cannot be formally decided. One might say that they are "intuitively" recognized as true.

But such an intuition has nothing to do with the *Urintuition* of the two-ity; it is equally unrelated to the intuitions invented by the philosophers. In this context, "intuitive" means semi-systematic or semi-axiomatic, or perhaps pre-axiomatic; it is synonymous with "naïve" as used, for instance, in the phrase "naïve set theory" as opposed to "axiomatic set theory." Consequently, Gödel's work on formally undecidable arithmetical sentences may be construed in the following trivial way: "The more restrictive your techniques of proof are, the less you will prove."

As Nagel and Newman point out,

"Gödel's proof should not be construed as an invitation to despair or as an excuse for mystery-mongering. The discovery that there are arithmetical truths which cannot be demonstrated formally does not mean that there are truths which are forever incapable of becoming known, or that a "mystic" intuition (radically different in kind and authority from what is generally operative in intellectual advances) must replace cogent proof." [33]

The intuitionist cannot make much out of the partial failure of the formalist program of endowing mathematics with definitive certainty by means of the axiomatic method and finitist procedures. The existence of formally undecidable true propositions proves neither the existence of pure intuition nor the necessity of adopting a logic based on the theory of knowledge. What the intuitionist can rightly demand, on the other hand, is that, *besides* formal logic, a methodological logic be worked out which elucidates and formalizes the pragmatic expressions "Demonstrable p," "Undecidable p," "Refutable p," "Plausible p," "Corroborated p," and their relatives, all of which occur in the language about scientific hypotheses. And it can be granted that intuitionists, because of their aposterioristic attitude in logic—which contrasts with their mathematical apriorism—are better prepared to undertake this task than both formalists and logicists. The latter are interested in reconstructions and completions of available material rather than in fresh starts and in processes.

Mathematical and philosophical intuitionism

There are, to be sure, further theses of mathematical intuitionism. But they are either subsidiary to those already examined, or they are too obviously inadequate. Of the seven

---

[33] Nagel and Newman, *Gödel's Proof* (1958), p. 101.

theses we have examined only one—the fourth, relative to the alleged intuitive origin of the most secure notions—is definitely intuitionistic in the philosophical sense. The remaining theses are shared by many mathematicians, logicians, and philosophers belonging to other camps, or to none. This is particularly true with respect to the intuitionist conception of mathematical research.

Whoever has done some mathematical work will admit that its dynamics is constructive, that the mathematician does not grasp ready-made Platonic Ideas, and that axiomatics is almost always an a posteriori reconstruction.[34] Hilbert, the champion of axiomatics, readily granted "the high pedagogic and heuristic value of the genetic method." [35] But he stressed the point that the axiomatic method is preferable "for the definitive presentation of our knowledge and its complete logical safety." (Had he lived a few years more he might have deleted "definitive" and replaced "complete" by "maximal.") And the Bourbakian Dieudonné states that axiomatic reasoning usually comes after intuitive reasoning, which is characteristic of periods of growth, "until the next revolution, which brings some new idea." [36]

The adoption of the axiomatic method is no longer a characteristic peculiar to formalism and logicism. It is so widespread that even intuitionist mathematicians employ it. The differences between the latter and nonintuitionists, with regard to the use of the axiomatic method, seem nowadays reduced to the following points: (a) intuitionists contend, and rightly so, that *no formalized system exhausts a theory*, because there always remains a residue of ambiguity in the interpretation of signs[37]—and, let us add, because every theory has a number of

---

[34] See, Courant and Robbins, *What is Mathematics?* (1941), pp. 88 and 216.
[35] Hilbert, *Grundlagen der Geometrie*, Appendix VI (1900).
[36] Dieudonné, "L'axiomatique dans les mathématiques modernes" (1951), pp. 47-8.
[37] Heyting, *Intuitionism: An Introduction* (1956), p. 102. The ambiguity and vagueness of signs, even of basic logical signs such as "not," was pointed out by the eminent logicist Russell in "Vagueness" (1923). But the consequence noticed by Heyting does not seem to have been realized.

presuppositions which cannot all be unearthed, simply because we are not aware of them all; (*b*) intuitionists, also rightly, do not believe that axiomatization is a *definitive logical warrant*. Even formalization, which adds the statement of the rules of formation, transformation, and designation to the explicit statement of the postulates and the listing of the primitive concepts, is far from providing a final crystallization. The intuitionist evaluation of the axiomatic method seems more realistic than the formalist appraisal, since complete formalization, as Gödel proved, does not provide definitive validation. On the other hand, intuitionists are misguided in seeking safety in "pure intuition," since there *is* neither pure intuition nor complete safety.

As to constructivism, it should be borne in mind that formalists and logicists are constructivist as well, though in their own way. Formalists are constructivists in that they try to restrict the foundations of formal systems to a finite number of terms and finitist procedures of proof (Hilbert's famous *finite Einstellung*). And logicists are constructivists in that they refuse to accept the introduction of new mathematical entities by postulation. They refuse to accept the contextual definition of mathematical primitives and try to reconstruct them with purely logical means (e.g., with the sole help of set theoretical predicates, such as "belongs to," or "is included in").

The main difference between intuitionist and nonintuitionist constructivism is that the former does not attempt to reconstruct mathematics with logical units (or to "reduce" mathematics to logic, as is usually said in a misleading way). Another difference is that intuitionists do not admit expressions such as "for all properties," which occurs, for instance, in the statement of the principle of mathematical induction.[38] In this sense, intuitionist constructivism is less daring than formalist constructivism, and the latter less than logicism. It is also more naïve than the latter, because it admits the existence of "immediate notions," or intuitive concepts, which are in no need of elucidation.

[38] See Carnap, "Die logizistische Grundlegung der Mathematik" (1931).

Mathematicians and metamathematicians have not, however, kept within the limits of the finitist constructivism of Hilbert and Brouwer. Thus the procedure of nesting intervals, so often used in set theory and in analysis, involves infinitely many steps. The Bolzano-Weierstrass theorem ("Every bounded infinite point set has at least one point of accumulation"), which has been called "the supporting pillar of the whole of analysis," [39] is proved by that procedure. Besides, transfinite inference modes have been devised which have enabled us to demonstrate new theorems and to prove propositions that were undecidable with weaker, finitist methods (see *The excluded middle*). Elementary statements in arithmetic, which were formerly justifiable in a semirigorous form, can now be validated with the help of more powerful tools, which is a complete reversal of the intuitionist and formalist ideal of reaching the complex and unintuitive through the simple and intuitive. As so often happens, life overflows the dikes erected by the schools.

PROS AND CONS

What remains of the intuitionist heresy? Our evaluation of this movement, a trend which is conservative on some counts and renovating on others, yields the following:

(1) *The intuitionist metaphysics, taken from Kant, is obscure and irrelevant to mathematics.* In particular, "the basal intuition of two-oneness," or of the sequence of natural numbers, is *not* an intuition; if it were, man would have built arithmetic hundreds of thousands of years earlier than he actually did. Even if it were an intuition and not a laborious logical construction that need not be regarded as finished, this would concern the psychology of mathematics and not pure mathematics.

(2) *Intuitionist mathematics and logic are counterintuitive.* They are so subtle and complex, and they require such ingenuous tricks, that very few master them, this being one of

---

[39] Waissmann, *Introduction to Mathematical Thinking* (1951), p. 196.

the reasons that they find no application. It has even been said that they "are so complicated that they are utterly useless." [40] Thus, for example, the intuitionist propositional calculus has four primitive operations instead of two, and eleven postulates instead of the four usual ones; besides, it prohibits the simplification of double negation, since the statement "It is absurd that p be absurd" is not equivalent to "p is true." (On the other hand, "It is false that p be *false*" is equivalent to "p is true.") The intuitionist set theory replaces the predicate "is denumerable" by six different predicates bearing almost untranslatable Dutch names. It may be that this theory is more analytic than the conventional set theory; but then why call it "intuitive"? In ordinary arithmetic, if a and b are real numbers and $ab = 0$, it follows that $a = 0$ or $b = 0$; in intuitionist arithmetic this proposition cannot be proved before showing that either $a = 0$ or $b = 0$. In ordinary logic and mathematics, whenever we face a problem without a sufficient equipment of premisses we may try the method of indirect proof, because we can introduce the negative of the conclusion as another premiss[41]; but this we are forbidden to do by intuitionist constructivism. Where is the physicist or the physiologist who is prepared to accept such weak and unintuitive logic and mathematics?

Besides, among intuitionists themselves there are disputes concerning the clarity of notions as important as negation and contradiction, which are not accepted as primitive by Griss, who champions a negationless logic. In such a logic the *modus tollens* (If p, then q; now, not-q; hence, not-p) cannot occur, so that it cannot be used as a tool for refuting hypotheses by means of counterexamples.

(3) *Intuitionist mathematics and logic depend upon the respective "classical" discipline.* They are not entirely new contributions but rather *re*constructions of available material. If "in order to build up a definite branch of intuitionistic mathematics it is necessary, in the first place, to have a thorough

---

[40] Curry, *Outlines of a Formalist Philosophy of Mathematics* (1951), p. 61.
[41] See Suppes, *Introduction to Logic* (1957), p. 41.

knowledge of the corresponding branch of classical mathematics," [42] as Heyting honestly admits, then the "basic intuition" cannot be as fertile as advertised.

(4) *The intuitionist requirements mutilate an important part of modern mathematics,* in particular, of the theory of infinity and of the theory of real functions. The results of intuitionist mathematics are contained in ordinary mathematics. The intuitionist methodology drastically restricts the freedom of mathematical creation (remember, on the other hand, Cantor's famous dictum: "The essence of mathematics lies in its freedom"). Likewise, its partner in the philosophy of physics—operationalism—would force us to dispense with the deepest, the most fertile, and the most interesting physical theories, since none of them can be reduced to a set of operationally defined concepts.

Paradoxically enough, intuitionism condemns as meaningless, or indemonstrable, or even false, a host of statements regarded as "intuitive" by the ordinary mathematician, such as, "Every real number is positive, negative, or zero," "Every set is either finite or infinite," and "Every function continuous in a closed interval has at least one maximum." By excluding a multitude of theorems that are usually regarded as "intuitive," mathematical intuitionism destroys itself.

(5) *Intuitionist logic is applicable to intuitionist mathematics only.* Intuitionist logic cannot be applied in factual science, since it denies the possibility of asserting strictly universal propositions unless they are conclusively demonstrated—which is imposible. In fact, in intuitionist logic the locution: "We assert that, for every x, x has the property P," means that $P(x)$ is true for every individual x of the universe investigated. This, in turn, means (by the principle of constructivity) that we have a method for proving that, if an arbitrary individual a of that universe ("species") is chosen, a has the property P.[43] But this is an impossible task in the interesting cases, which concern open classes.

[42] Heyting, *Intuitionism: An Introduction* (1956), p. viii.
[43] *Ibid.,* p. 102.

Besides, predictive statements should be banned from science if we were to submit to intuitionism, since only future events can render a prediction true or false in some degree. Yet, natural and social science can hardly be regarded as sciences if they do not yield predictions, the obtainment of which forces us to assign a *potential* truth value to predictive statements. If we want to calculate predictions, we are obliged to treat them *as if* they were capable of becoming true or false, but this is forbidden by intuitionism, which requires us to abstain from making unproved assertions. As a consequence, natural scientists employ nonintuitionist logic—which does not mean that they are entirely satisfied with it.

(6) *Intuitionist restrictions have been fertile in another direction:* they have stimulated the search for new, direct demonstrations of well-known mathematical theorems, as well as the reconstruction of previously invented concepts (e.g., real numbers).

New demonstrations are always welcome, especially if they show new connections; and new procedures for the formation of concepts are also welcome, especially if they contribute to their elucidation. But the intuitionist contributions do not compensate for the impressive body of theory which intuitionism asks us to sacrifice.

(7) *The intuitionist logic and philosophy of logic contain positive novelties.* In the first place, intuitionists, and particularly Heyting, have made a serious effort to build an epistemological logic capable of reproducing the actual course of scientific research. The shortcomings of what has so far been obtained should not count against the attempt itself.

In the second place, intuitionist logic has an interesting interpretation as a problem calculus.[44] In this model, due to Kolmogoroff (1932), the conditional "If p then q" is interpreted as: "Assuming that a solution of problem p is given, find a solution of problem q." The importance of the logic of problems cannot be exaggerated since, after all, every scientific work begins with some problem, and often ends by posing further questions. A

---

[44] See Wilder, *The Foundations of Mathematics* (1952), pp. 246-7.

further interpretation of intuitionist logic has been proposed by Tarski (1938), who has set up an isomorphism between the intuitionist propositional calculus and topology.[45] All this proves that intuitionist logic is both a consistent and rich system, not that it constitues *the* correct syntax of discourse.

In the third place, intuitionist logicians have gallantly posed once again the thorny problem of the *ground* for our choice among inference patterns, a question that may lack a definitive solution because it is not a purely logical but rather an empirico-logical problem. Experience alone, including the experience of mathematical work, can suggest reasons for adopting this or that inference pattern, this or that proof procedure and, in general, this or that system of logic. Logical *theories* are formal, but the choice among them depends not only upon logical considerations but also upon experience and upon our entire world view.

(8) *The psychology of mathematical invention favored by intuitionism is more realistic than the ludic or conventionalist theory,* because it recognizes that mathematical invention happens to be a mental process, because it is a dynamic, not a static, outlook,[46] and because it insists on the importance of nondeductive and informal elements in mathematical work. But these ideas are not the exclusive property of intuitionism; they have been held by evolutionists and materialists,[47] by pragmatists,[48] and by many isolated mathematicians before and after Brouwer.[49]

[45] Tarski, *Logic, Semantics, Metamathematics* (1956), chapter xvii.
[46] Black, *The Nature of Mathematics* (1933), sec. 3, has particularly insisted on this point, but he has overlooked the candor of the psychology of mathematical work as sketched by the intuitionists.
[47] See Struik, "Mathematics," in Sellars, McGill and Farber (Eds.), *Philosophy for the Future* (1949).
[48] See Dewey, *Essays in Experimental Logic* (1916).
[49] See Bôcher, "The Fundamental Conceptions and Methods of Mathematics" (1905) and Denjoy, "Rapport général" (1949). The latter is a remarkably violent attack upon Bourbakian formalism. The criticism of the Bourbakians was not any less virulent; witness Weil's complaint, in "L'avenir des mathématiques" (1948), p. 318, about the state of modern mathematics by mid-century in France, where "the extreme rigidity of a hierarchy [*mandarinat*] founded on anachronic academic institutions renders any renewal attempt, unless it is purely verbal, doomed to failure."

Besides, intuitionism is not historicist enough. It takes for granted that intuition is invariable and universal, to the point that "the concepts of an abstract entity and of a sequence of such entities are clear to every normal human being, even to young children" [50]—a statement which psychologists (particularly Piaget) and anthropologists would certainly dispute. As Freudenthal says,

Who is to decide the question of knowing what is intuitive? A savage, or a baby that have not yet been influenced by our geometrical civilization, or the average man, whose intuitive space has been molded by our straight streets flanked by parallel walls, and by the experience of all those products of technology that suggest to him the validity of the Euclidean axioms?[51]

With regard to the assertion that the "basic intuition" is pre-linguistic, it seems definitely inconsistent with the findings of contemporary psychology, according to which every thought is symbolical, i.e., accompanied by visual or verbal signs. Finally, the existence of Brouwer's "basic intuition" is at least as problematic as the existence of mathematical objects.[52]

We see, then, that mathematical intuitionism has both positive and negative elements. The former, the realistic elements, concern logic and the psychology of mathematics; the negative constituents, which are aprioristic and limiting, concern the "foundations" and methods of mathematics.

The debt of mathematical intuitionism to philosophical intuitionism is not large and, at any rate, what is involved is Kant's intuitionism and not the anti-intellectualist intuitionism of many Romantics and post-Romantics, although Weyl and Heyting have occasionally sought the support of quotations

[50] Heyting, *Intuitionism: An Introduction* (1956), p. 13.
[51] Freudenthal, "Le développement de la notion d'espace depuis Kant" (1959), p. 8.
[52] Curry, *Outlines of a Formalist Philosophy of Mathematics* (1951), p. 6.

from Husserl. Besides, the contacts between mathematical and philosophical intuitionism are precisely those which the majority of mathematicians would *not* accept. The working mathematician, if he is concerned with the philosophy of mathematics at all, does not sympathize with intuitionism, because it looks for an a priori foundation or justification, or because it praises an obscure "basic intuition" as the source of mathematical creation, or because it claims that such an intuitive foundation is the sole warrant of certainty. Mathematical and logical intuitionism are prized to some extent despite their peculiar dogmas, because they have contributed—though perhaps not as much as has Gödel's work—to the disintegration of alternative dogmas, particularly the formalist and the logicist ones.

Those who concern themselves with the so-called foundations of mathematics and logic (foundations the very existence of which ought to be questioned) no longer have the right to adopt the secure, triumphant, definitive tone of the formalists and logicists of the beginning of our century, who believed they had built infallible and consequently definitive "foundations." Mathematical theories are *hypothetico*-deductive systems. They do not start with certainties but with assumptions, i.e., corrigible statements, or at least with statements that can be reformulated and rearranged in the interest of consistency, depth, and fruitfulness. The propositions that are taken as basic in a given systematization are not incorrigible intuitions but tentative hypotheses, almost as tentative as in factual science. Gone are the days of perfect and secure foundations, and, perhaps, of foundations at all, as suggested by the rich interrelations of the various chapters of mathematics, and by the fact that the analyst does not worry about the difficulties faced by the set theoretician. Our theories, whether formal or factual, are not like buildings that crumble if their foundations are replaced; they are rather like growing organisms, with perishable and mutually controllable parts.

Mathematical intuitionism, then, has had the virtue of every new orthodoxy, namely, that of instilling diffidence toward the old orthodoxies. Another reason for the esteem accorded the intuitionists is their experimental or exploratory attitude toward the laws of logic and the problem of truth. And this experimental attitude, together with the opposition to dogmas which seemed immovable, are not precisely characteristic of philosophical intuitionism but bring logical intuitionism close to materialism, empiricism, and pragmatism. Consequently, the name adopted by Brouwer's school is largely an unfortunate misnomer.[53]

[53] Professor Heyting has agreed to this conclusion in conversation with the writer (1960).

3

THE SCIENTIST'S
INTUITIONS

KINDS OF INTUITION

A fable about method

Not a few philosophers are responsible for the widespread fable that scientists have two separate, well-trimmed and standardized methods by means of which they can approach any problem of knowledge. These methods are the deductive and the inductive procedures, which, presumably, enable scientists to do without hunches, trials, and, possibly, without talent, too (as Bacon thought they could if only they adopted his rules). According to this fable, the mathematician need do nothing but "deduce necessary conclusions from clear premisses"; yet no "method" is provided for obtaining the premisses.[1] And the physicist—if we are to believe the religion of method—need just summarize in inductive generalizations the results of his observations; but it is not said why he makes such observations or how he manages to design them and interpret their results.[2]

Few things are more inept and ridiculous than this cartoon of scientific work. Whoever has done something in science knows

[1] Against this distortion see the protests of Bernard, *Introduction à l'étude de la médecine expérimentale* (1865), pp. 85-6; Bôcher, "The Fundamental Conceptions and Methods of Mathematics" (1905); Klein, *Elementarmathematik vom höheren Standpunkte aus* (1911-14), I; Poincaré, *Science et méthode* (1908), Book I, chapter iii; Polya, *Mathematics and Plausible Reasoning* (1954): a complete and admirable work devoted to destroy the myth that deduction is sufficient in mathematics.

[2] The most vigorous indictment of inductivism will be found in Popper's *Logic of Scientific Discovery* (1935, 1959).

that the scientist, whether mathematician, naturalist, or sociologist, makes use of *all* psychical mechanisms, and that he cannot control them all and cannot always ascertain which has functioned in every case. In any scientific work, from the search for and statement of the problem to the control of the solution, and from the invention of the guiding hypotheses to their deductive processing, we find the perception of things, events, and signs; imagery or visual representation; the formation of concepts of various degrees of abstractness; the comparison which leads to analogy, and inductive generalization alongside the wild guess; deduction both informal and formal; rough and refined analysis; and probably many other ways of forming, combining, and rejecting ideas—because, incidentally, science is made up of ideas and not of facts.

When we do not know exactly which of the above listed mechanisms has played a part, when we do not remember the premises, nor have a clear consciousness of the inferential processes, or when we have not been systematic and rigorous enough, we tend to say that it has all been the work of *intuition*. Intuition is the collection of odds and ends where we place all the intellectual mechanisms which we do not know how to analyze or even name with precision, or which we are not interested in analyzing or naming.

The following are among the most frequently accepted uses of the term "intuition" in contemporary scientific literature: quick perception, imagination, abbreviated reason, and sound judgment.[3] Let us analyze them.

Intuition as perception

(1) *Quick identification* of a thing, event, or sign.

Clearly, the apprehension of a physical object, that is, sen-

---

[3] Poincaré, in *La valeur de la science* (1906), pp. 20 ff., distinguished four kinds of intuition: (*a*) the appeal to the senses and to the imagination (the latter being mainly the capacity for visual representation); (*b*) inductive generalization; (*c*) the intuition of pure numbers (which would yield the principle of mathematical induction—a principle which, incidentally, can be demonstrated); (*d*) over-all vision.

suous intuition, depends upon the subject's sharpness of perception, memory, intelligence, experience (the microscopist sees many things that elude the layman), and information (by and large, we do not perceive what we are not prepared to discover). Sensorially obtuse, or inexperienced, or just silly subjects are not good observers. Their sensible intuitions are inexact, that is, their discriminatory power—their ability to identify—is small.

Notice the limitation of sensible intuition: it gives us what in German is called *Kennen*[4] and what Russell called *knowledge by acquaintance*,[5] i.e., direct and unarticulated prehensions of singular concrete objects. Sensible intuition is but a raw material for *Erkennen, or knowledge by description,* or inferred knowledge; sensible intuition is, therefore, prescientific: it occurs in the work of the *scientist,* not in science as a product of that work. Scientific knowledge is not perception but the elaboration and transcending of perception.

(2) *Clear understanding* of the meaning and/or mutual relations of a set of signs (e.g., a text or a diagram).

It is in this sense that we say of an author that his descriptions and explanations are intuitive, or intuitively clear: his ideas are couched in terms that are simple and familiar *to us;* or he resorts to illustrations and metaphors that dig up something in our memories and excite our imagination. In the same way, we say that we understand intuitively a deductive chain as a whole, even though some link may escape us. Moreover, we judge that a chain of reasoning lacks "demonstrative force," from a psychological point of view, if it is too long or involved; this will happen, for instance, if the reasoning is interrupted by the demonstration of many auxiliary propositions (lemmas), or if the logical analysis has been pushed too far for our present needs.

It goes without saying that the clear grasp of a set of symbols will depend not only upon the symbols themselves—which may be clumsy and ugly like Gothic characters, or clean and sug-

---

[4] See Schlick, *Allgemeine Erkenntnislehre* (1925), p. 77.
[5] Russell, *Mysticism and Logic* (1918), chapter 10.

gestive like Latin initials—but also, and even mainly, upon our own ability and training. The beginner will "intuit" certain objects, but the specialist will seize, in addition, certain relations and complexities which the novice will miss.

Since what is characteristic of the formal approach to mathematics and logic is the insistence upon relations or structures rather than upon relata or entities, it is possible to say that the specialist in abstract structures, such as groups, evolves an intuition in handling them, which is a learned way of saying that he becomes *familiar* with such abstract structures.

Notice that what is psychologically obvious need not be logically straightforward. There are quite "obvious" theorems the statement of which can be understood by schoolboys, but which are very difficult to demonstrate—witness many theorems in number theory. And some relations are "obvious" (that is, psychologically simple) even though they are difficult to analyze —witness the relation of simultaneity. Therefore, there is no worse trap than the innocent-sounding "obviously," "naturally," "it is easy to see," and "it follows immediately," for they often hide difficulties, and sometimes these difficulties have not been solved by the authors of these little phrases.

(3) *Interpretation ability:* the ease with which the correct interpretation of artificial signs is accomplished.

We speak of persons who have "physical intuition" and of others who lack it. The former "see" in formulas—as long as they are not too complicated—something more than mathematical signs: they understand their physical meaning; they know how to read the equations in terms of properties, events, or processes. Thus, the theoretical physicist will tend to read the square of a magnitude as a candidate for some form of energy, a matrix as a table of possible transitions among different states, a Fourier integral as a wave packet, an expansion in orthogonal functions as a superposition of states, a commutator such as $HA-AH$ as a rate of change, and so on. A skill for symbolization, a certain amount of experience in interpretation, and a capacity for quickly establishing relationships among apparently disconnected items is all that the word "intuition" conveys in this case.

Not only physicists but also mathematicians develop a certain ability to interpret artificial signs. It is easier to construct first a concrete theory, whose basic (primitive) terms have a definite meaning, and then eventually eliminate such specific references, thereby obtaining an empty shell, an abstract theory, than to proceed the other way round. The abstract theory can then be given diverse alternative interpretations, among them the one that gave it birth. Such a freedom from specific reference has the advantages of disclosing the essential structure of the system (see *Husserl's Wesensschau*, Chap. 1), as well as having the greatest possible generality. An empty shell can be stuffed with a variety of contents or meanings.

Thus, for example, probability theory was first developed as a theory of expectations, i.e., as a psychological theory, and as a theory of contingent events, i.e., as a physical theory. Even nowadays most elementary textbooks on probability still speak of probabilities only in terms of beliefs or events. But the specialist realizes that these are only two among various possible *interpretations* of a theory that should be expounded as an abstract or uninterpreted system.

The expression "$P(x,y)$" occurring in probability theory may be interpreted, for example, as "the probability of the hypothesis x on the evidence y," or as "the probability of the chance event x in the sequence of similar events y," as well as in other ways, or in none. The consideration of probability theory as a semantic (interpreted) system has had a definite heuristic advantage: it is easier to think in specific terms, and particularly in visualizable terms, such as "event." On the other hand, these specializations have definitely obscured the very nature of the theory of probability. In particular, they have fostered the famous misinterpretations of probability as "nothing but" a logical relation, hence of the theory itself as a branch of logic, as well as the interpretation of probability as "nothing but" a limiting frequency of events, hence of the calculus of probability as a natural science.

A similar attachment of geometers to figures and bodies fostered the belief that geometry is the science of physical space (recall the very phrase "solid geometry") and hampered the development of non-representational geometries. Interpretation ability is a wonderful crutch. But who would prefer crawling with the help of crutches if he had the possibility of running?

Contrary to current opinion among semanticists, the author thinks that the capacity for interpretation cannot be mechanized or trivialized by simply explicitly stating all the rules of designation and interpretation postulates that confer a meaning upon the symbols concerned. A reason for this is that such rules and postulates do not *exhaust* meaning; both the body of presuppositions of the theory and its ulterior development contribute to its meaning. Besides, every symbol is surrounded by an aura of vagueness, no matter how many efforts are made to specify its meaning in a unique way.

The sum total of a body of knowledge, and even some adjoining areas, may unambiguously specify the meaning of its descriptive signs, or subject-matter constants. Even so, the operation of interpretation is not mechanizable, as shown by the difficulties so often encountered in the interpretation of results neatly derived from the assumptions of an otherwise well-known theory. If the business of interpreting a formalism were as straightforward as most semanticists imply it is, there would be no trouble in interpreting the formulas of, for instance, the quantum theory.

The rules of designation and the postulates of interpretation fix the use of the terms in a system, briefly describe their meaning, and partially determine it. But the whole content of a system of signs is given by the theory's presuppositions, by the general relations it contains (e.g., the law statements), and by the specific empirical information (e.g., numerical values) which the theory can absorb.

Consequently, the process of interpretation, which is interminable, can be described as logical, though not as entirely deductive, to the extent that it makes use of the logical relations existing among the terms of a given piece of discourse. It is only the relation between certain constructions (symbols, concepts, propositions) and the corresponding sensory experiences that is not logical but rather "intuitive," as Einstein remarked. But, of course, such relations do not belong to scientific theory; they only occur in the validation and application of scientific theory.

It will be noticed that the legitimate employment of the interpretation ability has been restricted to *artificial* signs, thereby excluding the intuition of the "meaning" of natural signs from the field of science. It is true that we often assess the "meaning" of complexes of natural signs, such as a person's appearance, postures, and gestures, in a quick and synoptic way. This is what we do whenever we give a personality report on the basis of only an interview. But the fact is that such "impressionistic" or intuitive diagnoses are too often wrong. No scientific psychologist would dare draw a personality picture with the sole help of an interview. The intuitive interpretation of *natural* signs, without the help of tests and theories, is as misleading in psychology as it is in physics; therefore it does not belong to science, or, if preferred, it is a protoscientific activity.

Intuition as imagination

(4) *Representation ability* or geometrical intuition: skill for the visual representation or imagining of absent objects, as well as for building images, visual or dynamic replicas or patterns of abstract entities.

Representation ability may be regarded as a specialization of the interpretation ability treated under (3) above. The so-called geometrical intuition, or spatial intuition, is precisely the ability to (*a*) form geometrical concepts (e.g., of a curve) by abstraction out of sensible intuitions (e.g., of a physical band or chord); and (*b*) associate arithmetic, algebraic, or analytic concepts with geometrical shapes.

The origins of mathematics, as well as its elementary teaching, are intimately connected with geometrical representation. But so are also most attempts at organizing abstract material. Thus philosophical discourse can often be clarified with the help of diagrams. As he departed from phenomenology and evolved to a kind of realism, Nicolai Hartmann became more and more fond of diagrams to illustrate his ideas; his *Einführung in die Philosophie* is profusely illustrated with line drawings.

Think of the psychological conviction that is attained if the operation rules of arithmetic and algebra are correlated with geometrical operations. For example, in order to "show" (though not to demonstrate) the equality $(a + b)(c + d) = ac + ad + bc + bd$, we may draw a rectangle of sides $a + b$ and $c + d$ and bisect the first side into the segments a and b, and the second into c and d. The figure will then immediately suggest the validity of the equality in question through the "identification" of the invisible products ac, ad, etc., with the areas of the visible regions of the drawing. Actually there is no identification but one-one correspondence; yet it is didactically more effective to speak of identification.

When a function is studied with the help of its graph, one resorts to the so-called geometrical intuition. We lean on it even when we search for a preliminary decision about the convergence of an integral. One of the author's most rewarding experiences when he was in prison, deprived of paper and pencil, was to imagine the behavior of a number of integrals depending very sensitively upon certain parameters. This visualization helped him to solve problems he had been wrestling with unsuccessfully for a long time. Similarly, the Argand-Gauss diagram for complex numbers, the level lines for functions of a complex variable, and the integration circuit are all visual auxiliaries that can be dispensed with in a formal reconstruction. But why should we dispense with them during the construction period if they are as fruitful as the Euler-Venn diagrams in class calculus?

When Newton (1642-1727) called our functions "fluents" and our derivatives "fluxions," he established a correlation among analytical entities and kinematical variables (position and velocity), which served him as a powerful heuristic resource. We tend to say that he worked intuitively, although Berkeley (1685-1753) complained, in *The Analyst*, that the fluxions of order higher than the first could not exist since they were not intuitable. Geometrical and kinematical intuition—of people trained in mathematics and in physics!—have played a very important role in the invention of calculus, in the derivation of true theorems, and also in the concealment of logical difficulties that were overcome later on in the nonintuitive reconstruction (the so-called arithmetization of analysis).

The limits of geometrical intuition have often been pointed out (see *Mathematical and philosophical roots,* Chap. 2). We grasp intuitively the discontinuities of a function and of its first derivative, since the former have a visual correlate in the jumps of the functions's graph, and the latter are visualized by the sudden deviations of the tangent. But it is almost impossible to "perceive" the discontinuities of second-order derivatives, associated with sudden changes in the curvature radius; and for derivatives of a higher order it is simply impossible to conclude anything about continuity with the sole aid of sight. Also, it is easily "seen" that the integral of sin kx between minus and plus infinity is zero, because the areas of the successive half-waves compensate for one another; but, then, why do we not "see" that the similar integral of cos kx may yield infinity (for $k = 0$), although the two functions differ only by a phase shift?

In a large part of his task, the mathematician cannot base his abstract reasoning on visual intuitions and on the geometrical intuition based upon them. But here, too, differences of background and personality play a part. Younger generations of mathematicians handle complicated relations without employing diagrams, whereas older generations would think that the work with relations always *requires* the use of concrete models. The philosopher Reichenbach went to the extreme of asserting that "it is quite impossible to think abstractly about relations," from which he concluded that the use of graphs in geometry is not merely a matter of convenience but "rests on a basic necessity of human thinking." [6] We should be careful not to assign our own personality traits and personal experience to immutable necessities of human thinking in the style of traditional rationalists.

Geometrical and kinematical intuitions appear also, of course, in physics, where it is usual and profitable to build visual models of several kinds. It is fashionable, however, to maintain that contemporary physics is intuitionless and even thoroughly counterintuitive, in the sense that it has forsaken the geometrical and kinematical models in the atomic scale. This is simply false.

The quantum theory in its usual interpretation—not so in various heterodox interpretations[7]—has abandoned corpuscular models of the sort imagined by Dalton and kinematical models like Bohr's planetary model of the atom. Quantum mechanics does not speak of minute marbles moving along perfectly definite trajectories. On the other hand, it does employ *alternative* intuitive auxiliaries, such as the probability cloud (the bread and butter of theoretical chemists, who call them molecular orbitals), the charge distribution (e.g., within the proton and the neutron), Feynman's scattering graphs, the shell nuclear model, and countless other models.

What is new in the visual auxiliaries of quantum physics, relative to the visual models of classical physics, is (*a*) that they do not all purport to picture *individual* objects and events, but rather statistical distributions of properties (e.g., mass,

[6] Reichenbach, *The Philosophy of Space and Time* (1928, 1958), p. 107.
[7] For a survey of the many heterodox interpretations of quantum mechanics that have been proposed in recent years, see Bunge, *Metascientific Queries* (1959), chapter 9.

charge, velocity) among large aggregates of similar microsystems, and (b) they are not all *literally representative* of objective things and events; some of the images may be symbolical, non-figurative, and even (as in the case of Feynman's graphs[8]) mnemonic devices useful for computation purposes.

Be that as it may, the theoretical physicist and the mathematician alike do use visual images of one sort or another. When they do so, we tend to say that they think in an intuitive or pictorial way (the German *anschauliches Denken*). The theory of Hilbert spaces, in which both mathematicians and physicists are interested, can be developed without a single visual image; but it is advantageous to regard the base functions as coordinate axes in a space of infinitely many dimensions, and an arbitrary function as a vector in such a space. In this way, the quantum-mechanical postulate, according to which the measurement of a physical variable produces a reduction of the wave-packet representing the physical system, is pictorially called the projection postulate. It is visualized as the projection, by virtue of a measurement act, of the state vector into one of the axes of the function space.

Imaginary representation or visual phantasy—what Mach called *Phantasie-Vorstellung*—is a good crutch of pure reason but no substitute for it. It reinforces ratiocination psychologically, not logically. Visual models are not very useful in field theory and statistical mechanics, and sticking to the visual image will often obstruct generalization and the grasping of non-visualized qualities and relations. Properties such as mass, charge, and spin, can only be visualized symbolically: they do not fit into Descartes' program of reducing the whole of physics to *figures et mouvement*.

Yet, since every theory is a set of ideas representable by *signs* (verbal or visual), theoretical work always requires a capacity for interpretation and representation. The dichotomy Abstract/Intuitive, in vogue during the first half of our century

---

[8] This interpretation of Feynman's graphs is advocated in reference 7, chapter 10.

in connection with physics, is, therefore, incorrect. And, of course, it is simply a lie of nationalistic propaganda that the so-called "abstract" theories are semitic creations while the "intuitive" ones (meaning the good ones) are Aryan, as was maintained in the Third Reich.[9] What is true is that some people are "visualists" and others much less so, and that "probably every visualist tends to use many more images than he actually needs objectively to put his thinking through." [10] If most mathematicians of the older generations think with the help of vague images, as Hadamard's inquiry seems to have established,[11] why should physicists, chemists, biologists, and psychologists dispense with mental pictures? Let no one be despised or praised by the amount of visual imagery he employs, as long as he succeeds in advancing science.

(5) *Skill in forming metaphors:* ability to point out partial identities in kind or in function, or complete formal or structural identities (isomorphisms) among otherwise different objects.

Logical examples of metaphors are the analogy of disjunction and addition, and the similarity of alternation and branching (exploited in Beth's "trees"). A mathematical example is the similarity between function and vector spaces, and the ensuing conservation of a part of the vocabulary ("base vector," "scalar product," "orthogonality"). A physical example, the model of the atomic nucleus as a liquid drop (which, incidentally, was fruitful enough to accompany the research which led to the fission bomb). A cybernetic example, the similarity between computers and brains. And a psychological example, the resemblance between police repression and inhibition.

Who would doubt that metaphors are effective heuristic guides? The mere conservation of part of the vocabulary, when going from one field to another, suggests analogies that facilitate

[9] See Frank, *Modern Science and its Philosophy* (1949), p. 148.
[10] Bartlett, "The Relevance of Visual Imagery to the Process of Thinking" (1927), p. 29.
[11] Hadamard, *The Psychology of Invention in the Mathematical Field* (1945), chapter vi.

the exploration and understanding of the new territory. But, of course, we must always remember that we are handling analogies and not substantial identities: this is what the warning "Do not push analogies too far" means.[12] Otherwise we may end up by believing that computers *are* brains, just as once upon a time it was thought that heat and electricity were fluids because some fruitful analogies between them and liquids had been suggested and even worked out. To find what may be called the *breaking point* of analogies is as important as to set them up.

The systematic employment of metaphors of a spatial, physical, and social kind by psychoanalysis, Gestalt theory and allied speculations *in the place* of scientific constructs is, together with their methodological weakness, one of the obstacles which stand in the way of their recognition as scientific disciplines. First a function is compared to a thing (e.g., an organic whole, or a field of force) or to a person (e.g., the superego to a censor). The next step is to endow the simile with autonomy, e.g., to treat the id, the ego, and the superego, as persons inside the person. The metaphor is no longer regarded as a heuristic or didactic device that illustrates a conception, but as a conception itself, and even as the most convenient one.[13] In science, metaphors are employed in the process of generating and communicating ideas, but are no substitute for conceptual thinking, which is inescapable in science.

(6) *Creative imagination,* inventiveness, or inspiration. As opposed to spatial imagination, which associates visual images with given concepts and propositions, creative imagination is involved (to speak metaphorically) when new ideas are engendered seemingly without pain, without much explicit logic, and suddenly or almost so. Creative imagination is far richer than imagery; it does not consist in the ability to evoke sense impressions, and it is not restricted to filling gaps in the map

[12] For a criticism of the abuses of metaphor in the literature of cybernetics, see Bunge, *Metascientific Queries* (1959), pp. 148 ff.

[13] Pederson-Krag, "The Use of Metaphor in Analytic Thinking" (1956), where it is maintained that analogical expression is required by psychology.

supplied by perception. It is called creative because it is the ability to create concepts and conceptual systems that may correspond to nothing in the senses (even though they may correspond to something in reality), and also because it gives rise to unconventional ideas.

Every mathematician and every natural scientist will agree that without imagination, without inventiveness, without the ability to conceive hypotheses and proposals, nothing but the "mechanical" operations can be performed, i.e., the manipulations of apparatus and the application of computation algorithms. The invention of hypotheses, the devising of techniques, and the designing of experiments, are clear cases of imaginative operations or, if preferred, of intuitive actions, as opposed to "mechanical" operations.[14] They are not purely logical operations. Logic *alone* is as incapable of leading a person to new ideas as grammar *alone* is capable of inspiring poems and as theory of harmony *alone* is incapable of inspiring symphonies. Logic, grammar, and musical theory enable us to detect formal mistakes and good ideas, as well as to develop the latter, but they do not supply the "substance," the happy idea, the new point of view.

Yet the fruitful invention and the deep insight, which the intuitionist[15] and the gestaltist[16] so much commend, do not emerge *ex nihilo*. In science and in technology novelty is engendered by observation, comparison, trial, criticism, and deduction; there is no new knowledge that is not somewhat determined by prior knowledge[17] and that is not logically related

[14] The role of imagination in the design of experiments was emphasized by Mach in *Erkenntnis und Irrtum* (1905), chapter ix.

[15] See the harsh polemics of Borel against Couturat in "Logique et intuition en mathématiques" (1907). It was partly an argument between the deaf, because Borel was defending *sensible* intuition whereas Couturat was mainly attacking Bergson's *metaphysical* intuition.

[16] Thus Wertheimer, in *Productive Thinking* (1945), devotes all of chapter vii to the genesis of Einstein's special theory of relativity—without saying anything that cannot be found in a good history of science.

[17] This was one of Peirce's main arguments against intuitionism in "Questions Concerning Certain Faculties Claimed for Man" (1868), reprinted in *Values in a Universe of Chance*.

to it. (In general, the new is always rooted in the old.) Besides, one does not know that a guess is "happy" before testing it, and such work requires the logical elaboration of the guess.

The process of invention is usually erased in the final presentation of the theory, the technique, or the experiment. Axiomatic theories, in particular, have a forbidding appearance: they seem to be acts of creation out of nothing. But, of course, they are not. Any axiomatic theory is built on the basis of available knowledge and with the help of available concepts and techniques. One begins by mastering the existing material and the tools, just as an artisan begins by assembling the raw material and the implements. Then one tries to get a synoptic view of the field. Next one sets up the main desiderata the axiom system ought to satisfy; most of the desiderata will have to reappear as theorems deduced from the axioms. Not before this preparatory stage will the guesswork begin.

During the constructive stage some conjectures will "leap to the mind"; usually the simplest occur first, and, of course, eventually they are found too simple to be adequate. One immediately tests them, i.e., checks whether they satisfy the desiderata. If the latter are not fulfilled, one introduces a small modification in the axiom candidate; or one considers whether the unsatisfied desideratum is really correct or indispensable. In this process of adapting the stronger propositions (the axioms) to the weaker ones (the desiderata, or future theorems), the latter are not untouchable; they may be simplified in order to make the task at all possible. And the successive guesses may not form a sequence uniformly approaching the aim; there will be temporary halts and regressions. This process strongly resembles that of artistic creation, from the first rough sketch to the final retouch. But for some obscure reason, the literary people seem convinced that creation can only be found in the arts.

Once the axiom system is built, one checks again whether it yields the desired theorems and whether it satisfies such logical requirements as consistency. The whole process is one of trial and error guided by knowledge, both articulate and inarticulate, and by certain rules of theory construction. In science, trial and error is not "blind"—prerational—as it is among earthworms, mice, and other animals. It is often methodical rather than erratic; it is guided by goals and methods and controlled by what we know. Notwithstanding, the process of scientific invention is closer to trial and error than to the sudden "insight" that jumps out of nothing. "Flashes" do occur in scientific work, but only as events in the midst of a rational creative process rather than as unconditioned triggers.

It is absurd to hold that intuition is superior to logic with regard to invention. No scientific or technological invention is possible without previous knowledge and ulterior logical processing. Or shall we believe the fable of the sudden inspiration which allegedly lightened the gravitation theory in Newton's mind, as if there had not been the previous contributions of Kepler, Galileo, and Huygens, and the "calculus of fluxions" (necessary for the test of the theory), as well as Newton's own previous attempts?

The idea that creative thinking is the opposite of reasoning is as mistaken as it is widespread. If it were true that thinking is the more creative the more it owes to unconscious processes,[18] day-dreaming and, a fortiori, night-dreaming should be more rewarding than controlled thinking; and computation, which can be "mechanized" or automatized to a large extent, should be regarded as highly creative. Freud's thesis, that almost every mental process "first exists in an unconscious state or phase, and only develops out of this into a conscious phase, much as a photograph is first a negative and then becomes a picture through the printing of the positive," [19] seems to have inspired the technique of "brainstorming."

Brainstorming, adopted in recent years by several corpora-

---

[18] This is, in fact, claimed by Springbett, Dark, and Clake, "An Approach to the Measurement of Creative Thinking" (1957).

[19] Freud, *A General Introduction to Psychoanalysis* (1924), p. 305.

tions in the United States for the purpose of stimulating the genesis of ideas, involves gathering people together in an informal setting for the purpose of discussing and proposing solutions to some problem. This is done in a "free association" atmosphere, which encourages "free-wheeling" and strictly forbids criticism. The technique was tested—after adoption!—and apparently was found ineffective. A group of psychologists at Yale designed and performed experiments involving control groups, and concluded that brainstorming definitely inhibits creative thinking.[20] How could it be otherwise if criticism was suppressed in these sessions? The effective approach to problems is both creative and critical. Dreaming, which is uncritical, is also unproductive by itself.

A classical example of seemingly sudden invention stimulated by nonrational factors was the discovery of the benzene ring by Kekulé (1829-1896) in 1865. He himself described the event, though, unfortunately, twenty five years later, thereby running the risk of interpolating elements of phantasy. He was in Ghent, writing his textbook on chemistry; the work did not progress, and he turned to the fireplace and began to doze. Images of atoms—Dalton's atoms—began to gambol before his eye.

My mental eye, sharpened by repeated visions of a similar sort, now distinguished larger structures of varying forms. Long rows, frequently close together, all in movement, winding and turning, like serpents! [Up to that time the molecular structures hypothesized had all been linear chains. The dream started with conventional knowledge.] And see! What was that? One of the serpents seized its own tail, and the form whirled mockingly before my eyes. I became awake, as though by a flash of lightning. This time I spent the remainder of the night working out the consequences of the hypothesis. If we learn to dream,

[20] Taylor, Berry, and Block, "Does Group Participation when Using Brainstorming Facilitate or Inhibit Creative Thinking?" (1958).

gentlemen, then we shall perhaps find truth. . . . We must take care, however, not to publish our dreams before submitting them to proof by the waking mind.[21]

Notice that the "vision," "natural revelation," or "intuitive lightning," did not come out of nothing. Kekulé had been wrestling for a dozen years with the problem of the structure of benzene (C_6H_6). As so often happens in such cases, he even dreamt of molecular structures and in his dreams, he did what every waking scientist does: he *imaginatively varied the hypotheses,* or some of their constituents, by trying one after the other. The flash of inspiration came after many efforts, as a culmination of the stages of preparation and incubation, as Poincaré called them. The *éclair* came after trying many hypotheses, deducing their consequences, and comparing the latter with empirical data.

When the "illumination" is produced, all the elements of the hypotheses and a part of the relevant empirical evidence are present but are still disconnected or incorrectly connected. The synthesis that fuses them all in a short lapse into a correct shape, that "perception" of the interconnections constituting a whole, is *one* among many syntheses that are tried.

The synthesis of hunches and data may be false; it almost always is. It must be tested, and this is what Kekulé did as soon as he awakened. He did not believe in revelation but in hard work. In fact, the first thing Kekulé did when he awoke was to work out the consequences of his conjecture, to ascertain whether they matched the empirical information (physical and chemical properties of benzene). And he advised: Dream, *meine Herren,* but then check.

Dream and hypnagogic imagery (occurring in the waking-sleeping state) must be adjusted to data and canons before they can be regarded as members of a scientific system.[22] Unlike day-

---

[21] Apud Libby, "The Scientific Imagination" (1922).

[22] The psychologist may say that scientific imagination is *reality-adjusted,* whereas nonscientific imagination is *autistic.* See McKellar, *Imagination and Thinking* (1957).

dreaming and pseudoscientific vagary, scientific imagination is controlled; it is constantly checked by the effort to conform to the bulk of scientific knowledge. Compare Rutherford, the imaginative scientist, with Freud, the imaginative writer.

Creative imagination without logic leads nowhere in science. "Without long and patient deductions there is no fertile intuition," wrote Couturat in one of his memorable polemics against the conception of scientific research as a work of art created in the heat of an inspiration altogether alien to logic.[23] Many people have original ideas; only a few of them are true and, even so, they will not acquire scientific citizenship unless and until they have been worked out and made testable. Originality is a desirable characteristic of every new scientific theory, but the ability to survive severe tests is even more than desirable: it is mandatory.

Of course, there would be no time to test all our hunches. We first criticize them, trying to find counterexamples that will explode them. Moreover, what is tested is never a *first* intuition —always rough—but a product of its rational elaboration. Imagine the reaction of an experimental physics group director whom you ask to test a dream you had last night!

Intuition as reason

(7) *Catalytic inference:* quick passage from some propositions to other propositions, perhaps by skipping stages so rapidly that the premises and the intermediary processes are not noticed,[24] even though they may appear in a careful reconstruction.

Here we see reason at work in a global way—to speak metaphorically—and not analytically or discursively. It is the Cartesian intuition, which dispenses with intermediate links and abbreviates "long chains of reasons." This is why we sometimes

---

[23] Couturat, "Logistique et intuition" (1913), p. 266.

[24] In Cobb's *Foundations of Neuropsychiatry* (1952), p. 250, we find the following elucidation of "intuition": "Intuition can best be defined as reasoning from premises and by processes that are forgotten. It is an extreme example of what goes on in most reasoning."

speak of the self-evidence or sudden understanding of a reasoning.

But the premisses and the intermediary steps that have been skipped or forgotten are so many that only a trained mind can arrive in this way at likely conclusions. Intuition must be educated, and only a *highly logical* mentality is capable of achieving "the synthetic apperception of a logical relation or set of relations," which is how Couturat characterized intellectual intuition.[25]

(8) *Power of synthesis,* or global vision, or synoptic grasp: the ability to synthetize heterogeneous elements, to combine formerly scattered items into a unified or "harmonious" whole, i.e., a conceptual system.[26]

Power of synthesis—which should not be confused with incapacity for analysis—is characteristic of intelligent and well-informed persons, whatever their occupation may be. We find it in the painter as well as in the statesman and the philosopher. The artist imaginatively composes perceptions and ideas and produces an organized whole. The statesman, the scientist, and the philosopher organize ideas around a central nucleus, and sometimes they succeed in doing it with simplicity in some respect, and with a certain unity of style, in which case we say that they proceed with elegance. We say of the expert that he is able to "see" quickly the kernel of the subject and of the layman or the beginner that they get lost in the details.

We do not feel we "understand" an argument unless we can grasp it as a whole. What Hadamard said of himself is probably true of most people, namely, that "any mathematical argument, however complicated, must appear to me as a unique thing. I do not feel that I have understood it as long as I do not succeed in grasping it in one global idea and, unhappily, . . . this

---

[25] Couturat, *op. cit.,* p. 267.

[26] For a discussion of the notion of conceptual systematicity, see Bunge, "The Weight of Simplicity in the Construction and Assaying of Scientific Theories" (1961), Sec. 1.2.

often requires a more or less painful exertion of thought."[27] Synoptic grasp is not a substitute for analysis but a reward for painstaking analysis.

Power of synthesis, like catalytic reasoning, can be improved. In the beginning of his scientific career, the author often missed the kernel of his own work, which was supplied by his teacher, Professor Guido Beck. Frequently it was only after some time, perhaps even after delivering the paper, that the unifying idea and the purpose behind it became clear. We possess only what we make.

Teaching is a good way, not only to master a subject, but also to invigorate the power of synthesis. A good teacher conveys a global picture of his subject and shows the relative weights of its parts. Yet it must be conceded that not many acquire both a great analytic skill and a great power of synthesis. More often than not, we either skilfully polish a little idea, or fumble with an unbaked grand vision. Only geniuses have and work out grand visions.

(9) *Common sense:* judgment founded upon ordinary knowledge, without resorting to specialized knowledge or techniques; or judgment limiting itself to past stages of scientific knowledge.

We often start with ordinary knowledge and do quite well with common sense. But both, necessary as they are, are insufficient. Science is not a mere quantitative expansion of ordinary knowledge; it creates unheard-of concepts and theories, often counterintuitive and incomprehensible to the layman. Logic is not a mere refinement of common sense; it, too, faces problems and builds theories which in many regards are shocking to common sense, or at least are beyond its grasp.

Logicians and mathematicians have found that at certain crossroads the "logical intuitions" accepted by common sense fail. (Remember the paradoxes of infinite classes and of self-reference.) Common sense is shocked by laws such as "If p, then if

[27] Hadamard, *The Psychology of Invention in the Mathematical Field* (1945), pp. 65-6.

not-p, then p." Yet this statement is true; furthermore, it is one of the ways of stating the "self-evident" proposition "If p, then p or p." No less paradoxical is the equality $a^2 = 0$, which holds, for instance, for certain non-zero matrices.

The mechanics of fluids and rotating solids, field theories, and quantum mechanics, are full of "paradoxes," that is, of propositions inconsistent with common sense, accustomed as we are to handling macroscopic solids in slow motion. (Contrary to what Bergson thought, it is intuition, not reason, that is directly anchored to experience with solid bodies.) The modern ideas that bodies in a vacuum move by themselves, that cold is not the opposite of heat, or that electrons interfere with themselves, are further counterintuitive conceptions.

A person familiar with the Newtonian concepts of absolute space and time may find counterintuitive the idea that every uniform velocity can be "transformed away" (in thought) by the choice of a suitable coordinate transformation. But that same person, accustomed to visualizing space as a fixed frame, or as an all-pervading ether, may find "intuitive" the postulate that the velocity of light in a void is absolute, i.e., independent of any reference system. This is an axiom of the special theory of relativity which is incapable of being visualized or understood in common sense terms once one has grasped the concept of homogeneous and isotropic space, and the accompanying equivalence of all inertial systems. If the same person is then trained in the special theory of relativity, he will in turn find counterintuitive the assertion—belonging to Einstein's theory of gravitation—that accelerations can be absolute if they are produced by gravitational fields, since the latter cannot be transformed away (except locally) by any choice of coordinates and are therefore absolute in a sense.

Common sense can be educated by gradual steps, but the gain of some new intuition may be paid for by the loss of old, incorrect, intuitions. We feel satisfied once we have "intuitively" grasped a theory, once it has become commonsensical to us; but by the same token we will find it difficult to accept some competing theory making different demands on our "intuitions." The more a person is acquainted with a given theory and its accompanying mode of thought, the more difficult he finds it to adopt a rival theory involving a different mode of thinking.

The working out of a theory requires one's complete submission to the mode of thinking which it sanctions. But the criticism of a theory and the search for new, better theories, requires the abandonment of any single mode of thinking attached to what has finally become commonsensical. To a certain extent innovation in science consists of discovering *pseudoparadoxes*, that is, counterintuitive propositions that disagree with common sense, whether prescientific or scientific. If scientists had been afraid of "inconceivable," "irrational," or counterintuitive ideas, we would never have had classical mechanics (now commonsensical!), field theory, or evolution theory —which were all rejected in their own time for being counterintuitive.

Common sense is not static; it is gradually being enriched by science and technology. No concept is absolutely, inherently intuitive or counterintuitive; the degree of intuitability of a concept is relative to some background knowledge. Let us, then, avoid saying "x is intuitive," and prefer instead "x was found intuitive by y relative to z," where "x" denotes some ideal unit (concept, hypothesis, theory), "y" some subject, and "z" some body of cognitions, beliefs, attitudes, and valuations. And let intuition play its heuristic role, but prevent it from dwarfing the shaping of concepts.

Intuition as valuation

(10) *Sound judgment,* phronesis, discernment, or insight: skill for the quick and correct appraisal of the importance and worth of a problem, the likelihood of a theory, the feasibility and reliability of a technique, or the convenience of an act.

When the young scientist seeks the advice of the veteran investigator, he should not expect from him information or detail but, rather, the sound judgment that talented people acquire after many failures. Whenever problems, hypotheses, or procedures are weighed, value judgments are formulated. We say that such judgments are "reasonable," "sensible," or "sound," if they match the bulk of our knowledge or of our experience (which should include the recognition that "unsound" ideas may turn out to be correct). When such value judgments are formulated after a quick examination, and when they are successful, we speak of intuition. The price we pay for phronesis is a long string of failures.

Phronesis is valuable as long as it does not become frozen into authority, in which case it becomes frozenness. An extremely talented physicist, a Nobel prize winner, had specialized in turning down original ideas. Among the ideas he rejected violently were the spin hypothesis (which he afterwards adopted and developed), the violation of parity, and the search for hidden parameters affording a more fully deterministic account of microscopic phenomena. There is no infallible judgment as to the worth of ideas or of persons.

A FURTHER LOOK AT SOME VARIETIES OF INTELLECTUAL INTUITION

Intellectual intuition as a normal mode of thinking

We see, then, that "intuition" is an equivocal term even in science—or, rather, in the language about science. We also see that Kant's "pure intuition," Bergson's "metaphysical intuition," Husserl's "intuition of essences," and the mystic "intuition of the One" play no role in science. In the language by means of which we speak of science, "intuition" designates modes of *perception* (quick identification, clear understanding, and interpretation ability), *imagination* (representation ability, skill in forming metaphors, and creative imagination), *inferring* (catalytic inference), *synthesizing* (global vision), *understanding* (common sense), and *evaluating* (phronesis).

All of the above are *normal* modes of perceiving and thinking, even though some of them are found in a more completely developed state among scientists; they are, consequently, accessible to psychology. No mysterious intuition is needed for the study of the scientist's intuitions. That scientific psychology has not yet studied some of these abilities with the care they deserve[28] is not only due to the intrinsic difficulty of the subject, but also to the fact that the subject itself has long been the prey of charlatans. Only those scientists who are more curious than they are anxious to maintain their reputations will dare to trespass the game preserve of pseudoscience.

Further, no less important, inhibiting factors are the tenets of introspectivism, behaviorism, and inductivism. The belief that introspection (both subjective and by means of interrogatory) is *the* method of psychological research has very often been accompanied by the belief that intuition is a *primary* phenomenon in terms of which the remaining psychical processes must be explained. The belief that observation of overt behavior is *the* method of psychological research is accompanied by a reluctance to probe into mental phenomena which, like invention, cannot easily be objectified and controlled. And inductivism is a further stumbling block because it presents itself as the definitive solution to the problem of scientific construction and inference.

On the other hand, several scientists have studied the phenomenon of inspiration in themselves or in colleagues. Unfortunately, they have provided us with only little more than case histories which are sometimes accompanied by recipes for

---

[28] A gauge of the scarcity of studies in the field is provided by an examination of the *Psychological Abstracts,* an international reference index. Its section on "Thinking and Imagination" is one of the thinnest. During the years 1957-59 a total of 26,416 books and papers were recorded, only 277 of which, i.e., roughly 1%, dealt with the subject. If we consider only the strictly scientific papers, i.e., if the mainly literary articles and the arbitrary dream interpretations are not taken into account, the percentage might be reduced to one-tenth.

expediting intellectual delivery and catching its elusive products.[29]

It may therefore be worthwhile to take a closer look at the most interesting varieties of informal thinking, namely, creative imagination (see *Intuition as imagination*) catalytic inference and global vision (see *Intuition as reason*), and phronesis (see *Intuition as valuation*).

Creative imagination

We speak of creative imagination when we refer to the introduction of new concepts, the stating of new hypotheses, or the invention of new procedures or techniques—in short, when we have a *new* idea, even if the idea is new only relative to our stock of ideas. This is certainly not the intuition of philosophers, which allegedly *grasps* something that is assumed to exist prior to the subject. Creative imagination is a constructive operation whereby some new conceptual entity enters the world and enriches it.

That reason and experience do not suffice in scientific work, has often been remarked. Thus Claude Bernard, one of the founders of experimental medicine, said that the experimental method is based on the tripod of "feeling" (or sentiment), reason, and experience. He added that "feeling" always holds the initiative and engenders "the *a priori* idea [= *hypothesis*], or intuition." [30] Let us not reify functions and levels of the scientist's brain: it is sufficient to say that experience (actual and recalled), imagination, and logical processing, are among the necessary traits of the scientist's work.

The North American chemists Platt and Baker, in a re-

---

[29] See the studies of Poincaré, *Science et méthode* (1908), Book I, chapter iii; Hadamard, *The Psychology of Invention in the Mathematical Field* (1945); Platt and Baker, "The Relation of the Scientific 'Hunch' to Research" (1931); Cannon, *The Way of an Investigator* (1945); Dubos, *Louis Pasteur* (1950); Bartlett, *Thinking: An Experimental and Social Study* (1958); and Skinner, "A Case History in Scientific Method," in Koch (Ed.), *Psychology: A Study of a Science* (1959), Vol. II.

[30] Bernard, *Introduction à l'étude de la médecine expérimentale* (1865), p. 66.

markable empirical investigation of the role of the "hunch," or "scientific revelation," in research, defined it thus:

> A scientific hunch is a unifying or clarifying idea which springs into consciousness suddenly as a solution to a problem in which we are intensely interested. In typical cases, it follows a long study but comes into consciousness at a time when we are not consciously working on the problem. A hunch springs from a wide knowledge of facts but is essentially a leap of the imagination, in that it goes beyond a mere necessary conclusion which any reasonable man must draw from the data at hand. It is a process of creative thought.[31]

A total of 232 investigators turned in Platt's and Baker's questionnaires. One-third admitted having had intuitions ("scientific revelations") with some frequency in the solution to important problems; one-half said they had had occasional "revelations," and the remainder declared not to know the phenomenon by acquaintance. It would be interesting to repeat this investigation now that thirty years have elapsed and that the number and influence of scientists has increased at least by a factor of 10.

Both psychology and empiricist metascience, however, have neglected this aspect of scientific activity (see *Intellectual intuition as a normal mode of thinking*) by exaggerating on the other hand the role of sense data (and the corresponding observation statements), as well as the "collection of facts." This neglect implies that we have pure perceptions undisturbed by our theories and expectations, and that data are collected in science like postage stamps, just for the fun of it, and not in the light of theories and with the aim of widening and deepening our theories. Formalists, on the other hand, have exaggerated the importance of the final logical organization of acquired knowledge, without paying attention to the modes of inception of the premises.

[31] Platt and Baker: see footnote 29.

Empiricists and formalists seem to have been ashamed to recognize that the spark of scientific construction—the formation of new concepts, the "divination" of fresh assumptions, and the devising of new techniques—fits neither into the level of sense perception nor into the level of logical reconstruction, but must find a place in an intermediate level, equidistant from both the sensible and the discursive ones. They have expressed dislike for the term "creation," as if it involved emergence out of nothing, and have preferred to say that newness, whether in nature or in mind, is nothing but an illusion, a name for the division, rearrangement, or composition of previously existing units. One result of this philosophical preconception is that we scarcely have a theory of intellectual delivery.

Granted, nothing comes out of nothing. This is an important ontological principle variously illustrated in science, the denial of which leads to mysticism and indeterminism.[32] But why should we deny that there is invention, original mental creation out of perceptual and conceptual material, if we are prepared to grant that a chemical synthesis is not just a juxtaposition, and that a living being is not merely a complex mechanism?

Certainly, the famous alleged "insight" of Köhler and the other gestaltist psychologists does not solve the problem of intellectual creation: it just baptizes the difficulty. Moreover, insight occurs, if at all, after unsuccessful trials; it is a trial itself and is impossible without previously acquired experience. Köhler's thesis that flashes of insight are independent of previous experience was experimentally disproved in 1945 [33]; the importance of experience for "insightful" solutions has been established. Among higher animals, success in problem solving depends upon past experience, trial and error, and a more or less complex process of imagery and ideation.

The fact that "blind" or erratic trial and error are very inefficient does not establish the hypothesis of sudden creation out of

---

[32] See Bunge, *Causality* (1959), sec. 1.5.2.
[33] Osgood, *Method and Theory in Experimental Psychology* (1953), p. 613.

nothing, but rather the importance of conceptually organizing and enriching experience. Trial and error may be methodized in different degrees, the highest of which is the guess-test process occurring in science, in which every new guess is constructed out of material provided by the entire available body of knowledge, both direct and inferred.

The point is that the "insight" may provide a *synthesis* and not merely a rearrangement. The notion of centaur is certainly the result of a composition; but what about the concepts of temperature, of electric charge, of law of nature, or of the concept of concept: what are they composites of? In the vast majority of cases, we divide and conjoin and rearrange, we break up what has been together and bring together what has been separate. But on a few decisive occasions, man is capable of creating new concepts, new hypotheses, new theories, and new world views out of quite inferior raw material. Such moments we call creative.

In regard to creativity, thinkers might be classified in the following species: (*a*) *destructive critics,* i.e., persons able to find fault with other people's work but incapable of replacing the old and worn by something new and better; (*b*) *appliers:* individuals capable of using existing theories and techniques for the solution of specific problems, whether cognitive or practical; (*c*) *developers:* constructive critics who are able to extend or refine the known tools, yet along the same general line; (*d*) *creators* of new problems, new concepts, new theories, new methods, or even new ways of thinking. Science and philosophy needs them all.

William Whewell (1794-1866), a scientist, historian of science, and philosopher of science, was one of the few men living in the era of Comte and Mill who understood the nature of science. He insisted that the secret of scientific discovery is creativity in the invention of hypotheses and sagacity in selecting the correct one. "The Conceptions by which Facts are bound together," so he wrote one century ago, "are suggested by the sagacity of discoverers. This sagacity cannot be taught. It commonly succeeds by guessing; and this success seems to consist in framing several *tentative hypotheses* and selecting the right one. But a supply of appropriate hypotheses cannot be constructed by rule, nor without talent." [34] Every accepted hypothesis is a "happy guess," as Whewell called it; and, of course—as Poincaré remarked later on—guessing comes before proving.[35] But how many unhappy guesses precede the accepted one, and how unhappy is the ultimate fate of even the happiest of all! (This Whewell would deny, for he held the view that scientific progress is cumulative.)[36]

As Whewell saw, in the sciences, "There is a constant invention and activity, a perpetual creating and selecting power at work, of which the last results only are exhibited to us." [37] A look at some of the one hundred thousand or so scientific journals now in existence cannot fail to convince anyone of the creative imagination displayed in much of scientific research.

Those who praise the arts for being imaginative and deprecate the sciences for their alleged "aridity" cannot have gone beyond the logarithm table. It may be argued that scientific research is enormously more imaginative than artistic work, even though the ingenuity involved may not show up in the finished product. It may be argued that Einstein's photon hypothesis (1905), Oparin's hypothesis of the origin of life out of a primeval "soup" (1923), or the ENIAC, that wondrous handmaid of applied mathematics (Mauchly and Eckert, 1946), are each more ingenious creations than Michelangelo's *David,* Shakespeare's *Hamlet,* or Bach's *Passion according to St. Matthew.*

Creative imagination is richer in science than it is in the arts, because it has to transcend sense experience and common sense; and it is more exacting, because it has to transcend the self

[34] Whewell, *Novum Organum Renovatum* (1858), p. 59. See a vindication of Whewell in Schiller, "Hypothesis," in Singer (Ed.), *Studies in the History and Method of Science* (1921), pp. 426 ff. Schiller rightly corrects: instead of saying *the correct hypothesis* we should say *the best.*

[35] Poincaré, *La valeur de la science* (1906).

[36] Whewell, *History of the Inductive Sciences* (1858), I, p. 45.

[37] Whewell, *Novum Organum Renovatum* (1858), p. 65.

and must try to be truthful. Scientific research is not mere *Dichtung*, but tends to be *Wahrheit*. Yet some of its moments and some of its products, particularly the great theories that change our world outlook, are as poetic as poetry can be.

If the requirements of usefulness, reliability, profit, and low cost are superimposed on truth, we have modern technology. That technological invention is not in any sense inferior to scientific creation, and that it involves an equivalent exertion of phantasy and investment of knowledge, should be conceded by anyone not sharing the aristocratic contempt of work and artifacts.

The account of the creative process given by the engineer Rudolf Diesel does not essentially differ from Poincaré's famous account of his own invention of a certain class of functions. Diesel writes that

> An invention consists of two parts: the idea and its execution. How does the idea originate? It may be that it sometimes emerges like a flash of lightning; but usually after laborious searching it will hatch itself out of innumerable errors; and by comparative study will gradually separate the essential from the non-essential, and will slowly permeate the senses with ever greater clarity, until at last it becomes a clear mental picture.[38]

He is not able to ascertain whence came the idea constituting the kernel of his invention of the Diesel engine; he only knows that "from the incessant chase after the desired result [an aim clearly stated in technological terms], from researches into the relationships of countless possibilities, the correct idea was at length developed and I was filled with unutterable joy."

In engineering, just as in any branch of science, the ideal model first conceived will seldom fit into reality. A laborious and imaginative process of adjustments will be needed before a working model is produced. As Diesel says,

[38] Diesel, *Die Entstehung des Dieselmotors* (1913), in Klemm, *A History of Western Technology* (1959), p. 342.

. . . even when the idea has been scientifically established, the invention is not yet complete. Only when Nature herself has given an affirmative reply to the question, which the test has put to her, is the invention completed. Even then, it is only a compromise between the imagined ideal and the attainable reality. . . . An invention is never a purely mental product, but is the result of a struggle between thought and the material world. . . . It is always only a small part of the exalted ideas which can be established in the material world; and the completed invention always appears quite different from the original imagined ideal which will never be attained. That is why every inventor works amidst an enormous number of rejected ideas, projects and experiments. Much must be attempted for anything to be achieved. Very little of it is left standing at the end.[39]

In technology, as in science, the initial spark of intuition may trigger a chain reaction among pre-existent items of knowledge; but the end result is usually very different from the initial spark. At any rate, the creative imagination of the technologist or of the scientist does not operate in a vacuum; there is no scientific inventiveness or technological innovation without a set of data or outside a framework made of more or less articulated points of view. The creative imagination of scientists and technologists is not external to data, theories, desiderata, and even the general intellectual atmosphere. "Hunches" do not pop up by themselves, but in response to problems; and, in turn, the mere statement of questions presupposes a cognitive background in which holes have been noticed. Bohr and Edison could not have been produced by the Middle Ages.

The very test of a guess, a theory, or an instrument, is indebted to a whole body of informations, assumptions, criteria, and aims. Proofs, conclusive, as in mathematics, or imperfect, as in physics and engineering, are sketched with the help of tools

[39] Diesel, *op. cit.*, pp. 342-6.

supplied by theories and by logic, that theory of theories. And the weight of a proof is estimated with the help of methodological criteria.

In short, no science, whether pure or applied, is possible without creative imagination. The main difference between scientific imagination and artistic imagination is that the former faces more formidable tasks, such as the drawing of mental pictures of very complex non-sensuous objects, and must constantly be checked by theory and experiment.

Catalytic inference

What we have called catalytic inference (see *Intuition as reason*) takes part in the "anticipation" or "guessing" (surely incorrect more often than not) of results of laborious demonstrations or exacting empirical tests, which have no *Ersatz*. Catalytic inference consists in "showing" rather than in demonstrating: in proving in a brief and imperfect way, in rendering plausible the hypothesis that has been invented. The psychological force of catalytic inference derives from its brevity and from the reference of its terms rather than from its logical form. Catalytic inference is a kind of rudimentary reason that uses incomplete evidence, visual images, and analogies rather than complete data, refined concepts, and detailed inferences. Just because it is rudimentary and fragmentary, catalytic inference is unsafe.

It is paradoxical that intuitive reasoning should be preached as the way to certainty, since the safest course in developing information is careful analytic work. We make leaps when we are in a hurry, or when we are bored by the safest inference patterns, or when we do not know how else to proceed—never because the leap itself will generate a secure result. It takes years to teach children not to make wild guesses when deduction is possible; and it takes a further period of training in strict discourse before leaps can again be tried with some chance of success. In any case, whether we proceed step by step or by leaps and bounds, we employ "stored information" to produce the desired solution.[40]

The plausibility of an argument lies, for philosophical intuitionism, in the meaning or *reference* of its terms rather than in its logical *form*, because it is the former and not the latter that can be intuited. Therefore, two arguments with the same logical form may not have the same force for the intuitionist. Thus he may accept Descartes' *Cogito, ergo sum* (which is logically incomplete), but not the equally defective enthymeme: *He contradicts, hence he rejoices.*[41] The history of knowledge shows that fragmentary arguments, sometimes accepted because they hinge on intuitive notions, must either be abandoned as incorrect or must be logically reconstructed. Catalytic inference, praised by intuitionism because it is brief and readily accomplished and grasped, must be expanded to be validated.

Those who believe in the omnipotence of deductive logic are of the opinion that we could dispense with catalytic inference if only we had time, that with patience anything can be demonstrated by starting from adequate axioms and applying the suitable rules of inference. This belief is naïve. No table of axioms and rules of transformation constitutes an algorithm that can be applied "blindly"; it does not tell us which premisses we must choose, what auxiliary hypotheses we must frame, what transformations we must perform in order to demonstrate a given proposition.

A table of axioms is part of the raw material, and the rules are the tool for working on it, but neither of them is a guide. Having the axioms and the rules of inference is like having a fortune: to spend it we first have to fix certain desiderata, and then we must employ our imagination. (On the other hand, there is a simple recipe for *dis*proving any general proposition, namely, to produce a counterexample or unfavorable instance.)

Let q be a proposition obtained in no matter what way. (The

---

[40] See Bartlett, *Thinking: An Experimental and Social Study* (1958), p. 65.
[41] See Beth, "Cogito ergo sum—raisonnement ou intuition?" (1958).

way may not be proper, but at any rate the proposition itself is interesting or, at least, judged useful by somebody.) If we wish to demonstrate q in a constructive or direct way, we have to find a proposition p such that the further proposition "if p then q" be accepted as true; i.e., this conditional must either be an axiom of the system or a previously demonstrated theorem in it. Now the search for the proposition p that logically entails q is not a deductive process subject to precise rules and, therefore, mechanizable; it is, on the contrary, a somewhat erratic process. In order to perform the rigorous inference, both p and the conditional "If p then q" must be *found*—and no recipes are known for expediting this process. Add to this the fact that in a number of demonstrations in mathematics and physics singular or existential propositions must be constructed in addition to the universal premises. In mathematics, these are the celebrated tricks which must be invented in the decisive junctions and which, at one time, consist of special geometrical constructions, and, at other times, of special equalities or functions.

The search for the universal and particular premises needed for a rigorous deduction is not an automatic linear march but resembles somewhat the process of scanning that takes place in TV and, perhaps, in vision. The mind reviews, as it were, the stock of known propositions in the same field, and sometimes in related fields as well; it tries possible relations among such items, one after another in quick succession, until it discovers, if at all, the one that makes the demonstration possible. This scanning, however, is far more erratic and less efficient than the one responsible for TV images. To effect this zigzagging march there is no other useful rule than patience and the accumulation of fertile or suggestive relations. This process is "intuitive" to the extent that, despite being rational, it is not entirely conscious—or, if preferred, it does not fit entirely into the focus of awareness. Also, it does not adjust itself entirely to logical patterns; in the best of cases it does not break them.

In summary, it is not exactly true that formal logic could exhaust the study of demonstration.[42] What is true is that deductive logic is the *discipline* that codifies the *valid* relations holding among the *final* products of the demonstrative process; and this is why it can be called the *ars demonstrandi*. Nor is it true that logic is incapable of explaining the fact that nonrigorous, informal reasoning can be fruitful. A famous theorem of propositional calculus says that *any* proposition whatsoever, true or false, may be deduced from a false proposition: "If not *p*, then (If *p*, then *q*)". Both for the search and for the test of new ideas what is essential is *to get hold of some premiss,* rather than to adhere unimaginatively to the given assumptions.[43]

Phronesis

Finally, phronesis or sound judgment (see *Intuition as valuation*), although it does not enable us to decide conclusively between rival hypotheses, theories, and techniques, presents itself much like the Muses of antiquity: it would appear to be telling us in a faint voice which alternative is the most "reasonable" or the most viable. (Notice that there is no similar intuition for the assessment of costs of scientific projects.) Of course, the deaf have no Muses. In all its forms a highly developed intuition is neither a faculty common to the whole human species, nor an exclusive inborn characteristic of a few chosen people. It is rather the product of heredity, observation, learning, thinking, and evaluating.

Sound judgment is needed in the design of experiments no

[42] In his disgraceful war upon scientific logic, Poincaré had the weakness of granting that logic was "the instrument of invention." As a matter of fact, there is seldom a rigorous demonstration without a previous global vision of the process, nor is there invention alien to logical relations: the spark does not pop up in a vacuum.

[43] Even the so-called proofs without premisses, which occur in logic, require the extraction of the suitable premisses out of the proposition to be proved. Consequently, they should be called "proofs without premisses other than those supplied by the demonstrandum." Thus, to prove $(Ex)Fx \rightarrow -(x) -Fx$ we may choose as premisses the antecedent and the negation of the consequent of this same conditional.

less than in the practice of law. Quite apart from the ingenuity required in the planning of an empirical test, there is the question of estimating whether the chosen line of research is likely to be an effective way of attaining a given goal. We may have asserted a prediction with the help of a law statement and then may wish to ascertain whether the prediction will come true or not, in order to test the law statement; but in setting up the experiment we make a *further* prediction, namely, one concerning the value of the experimental setup itself. There are some criteria and rules of thumb for estimating designs of experiments, but there are no *laws* enabling us to predict the performance of the experiment itself. This prediction is largely a matter of phronesis, that wisdom which is our compensation for failures.

The psychologist Sir Frederic Bartlett, in dealing with the forecast of the adequacy of experiments, says that

> . . . something more is needed for good forecasting [of this kind] than wide knowledge and the successful practice of experiment. These must be combined with willingness to take a risk, and to move from evidence which opens up a lot of possibilities in some order of preferred direction. Because varied possibilities are always a part of the story, the forecasts must allow for adaptability in practice, and any experimenter who pursues them in the spirit in which they are framed must know early when to move away from one line and into another. . . . When everything has been said that can be in terms of extent and accuracy of knowledge, and practice in experiment, it still looks as if the successful use of this sort of prediction depends upon great sensitivity to positive properties of direction in the contemporary scientific movements, most frequently as these exhibit overlap with earlier movements out of which they have grown. When the forecast is made it is usually difficult, and often impossible, for the forecaster to say anything at all about the cues which he is using. If, however, he is able to compare practical lines of possible ex-

perimental development, and to assess in terms of probability either the odds that any of them will be followed, or that any will be successful, he must be able to identify at least some of his cues, and he must allege some knowledge about their relative weights. We come to this: that the capacity to identify ahead of anybody else, lines of experimental development which are "likely" to be fruitful, or "likely" to fail, depends upon evidence; but that it is by no means necessary that the person who uses this evidence should be able to say what the evidence is.[44]

The scientist gradually develops a "nose" for, or an "insight" into, the choice of problems, lines of investigation, techniques, and hypotheses. This "nose" is lost as a result of insufficient training, loss of interest, and prolonged concentration in routine tasks or in too narrow fields. (This is one of the reasons we should not work too many years on a single problem.) But the ability to evaluate ideas and procedures is not to be found among scientists alone; it is found in every sector of culture. Phronesis never occurs detached from either experience or reason; it is one of the few benefits of aging.

INTUITION: AN UNDEPENDABLE EMBRYO

Intuitions and their test

There is little doubt, in short, that intuitions of various sorts occur in scientific research, although they are absent from science as a body of propositions. But the scientist, though esteeming intellectual intuition because of its suggestive power, knows that it can be dangerous: first, because intuition has no demonstrative force; second, because intuition is partly ordinary common sense, and common sense is conservative; third, because intuition is never fine enough.

A hypothesis formulated in an intuitive way will have to be

---

[44] Bartlett, *Thinking: An Experimental and Social Study* (1958), pp. 156-7.

worked out in a rational way, and then tested by the usual procedures. Similarly, intuition may suggest the great links in a deductive chain, but does not save us the rigorous, or at least the best possible, demonstration. It may incline us in favor of one theory or technique over others, but a suspicion is not a proof.

The intuitionist philosopher puts an end to the most important part of his work once he has formulated what he regards as his "intuitions" (which he rarely has, busy as he is with praising the power of intuition and denouncing the limits of reason). The scientist, on the contrary, only *begins* a stage of his work with some "intuition," because he knows from experience that intuition is an undependable embryo.

It is a requirement of science that, in most cases, it be possible to validate *objectively* propositions and test procedures. Agreement may take long, but it is always sought and almost always found, even if transitorily, on the basis of previously accepted objective criteria. On the other hand, if an "intuitive" person has an intuition and another the contrary intuition, since both are of equal worth according to philosophical intuitionism, they will be equally exempt from every test, and the contradiction will remain unsolved. Of course, the *ad hoc* hypothesis may be made, and believed, that one of the *illuminati* possesses special properties as a consequence of which he must be believed above all others. Without resorting to such a principle of authority—the germ of the *Führerprinzip*—intuitionists have no way of making decisions between contradictory judgments. This is why philosophical intuitionism is a good companion of authoritarianism.

Scientists esteem intuition, particularly creative imagination, catalytic inference, and phronesis, but do not *depend* upon it. They know that psychological self-evidence is no warrant of truth, that intuition is highly personal, and that it often plays bad tricks. Intuition was invoked in favor of the claims that an infinite series cannot have a finite sum, that no geometry other than Euclid's could exist, that there is no curve without a tangent, and that the set of integers must be twice as numerous as the set of even numbers. Intuition was also invoked in support of the views that the length of bodies cannot be dependent upon their state of motion, that space and time are altogether independent of one another, that nothing could move of itself, that nothing might occur once the cause has ceased, and that there could be neither antipodes nor societies without private property, police, army, or religion. What characterizes scientific knowledge, besides logical organization and accuracy, is *testability,* and not self-evidence or subjective certainty, which are sometimes associated with intuition and so often shelter prejudice and superstition.

Intuitability is not a criterion for building and evaluating scientific theories. An easily intuitable theory is one built with *familiar* and, possibly, highly visualizable ideas. And such a theory will probably be too superficial and simple and will lack that desirable characteristic of new theories: originality. On the other hand, we are entitled to ask that the *presentation* of theories, however abstract, be "intuitive" to us, in the sense that it makes contacts with our fund of knowledge. But this is a didactic, not a scientific or metascientific requirement.

In science, self-evidence, that is, *psychological certainty,* must be distinguished from objective credibility or founded likelihood. Scientists know that nothing is epistemologically evident, however clear and true it may appear at first glance or to an expert. They know that sensible intuition may be defective or even altogether deceptive, this being a reason why sense data alone, without the control of instrument and theory, are not the ultimate criteria of empirical verification. Scientists know that there are no Cartesian "simple natures" which can be grasped once and for all, and that there exists no Husserlian "vision of essences" which can give us pure essences, the very existence of which should first be demonstrated.

Scientists know that truth is not produced by contemplation but by controlled imagination and planned doing, by the impatient invention and patient trial of guesses. They also know that the propositions and theories regarded as true at a given moment are, if they refer to facts, corrigible and perfectible. Scientists know, in one word, that conclusive self-evidence and ultimate foundation are not to be found even by the scientific method. As a consequence, they do not join intuitionist philosophers in their quest for final certainty and fundamentality.

"Intuitive" vs. "systematic"

The progress of science, both formal and factual, has consisted, to a large extent, in *refining, justifying,* or even *eliminating* the intuitive elements occurring in all theories before formalization. This process has occurred not only in mathematical analysis and in the theory of sets, where intuitive reasoning, operating with analogies with finite collections, had given rise to certain paradoxes; much the same happened in geometry and in mechanics, two disciplines that had traditionally been regarded as intuitive. When one intuition cannot be justified, or when it resists attempts at elucidation, it must either be eliminated or suspended, precisely because intuition deceives and hides as much as do the senses and induction. As Couturat said, "the so-called intuitive 'self-evidence' may conceal a mistake in reasoning or a postulate." [45]

In the context of analytic philosophy, it is customary to call intuitive those concepts, propositions, and demonstrations which have not yet been cleaned, elucidated, or reconstructed in an exact manner. Thus Quine says, "By an intuitive account I mean one in which terms are used in habitual ways, without reflecting on how they might be defined or what presuppositions they might conceal." [46] Such a procedure—the customary one—may be termed *semantically intuitive.*

There is also a mode of reasoning which is *syntactically intuitive:* the one that grasps more or less directly some logical relations, such as inclusion, contradiction, logical entailment,

---

[45] Couturat, *Les principes des mathématiques* (1905), p. 288.
[46] Quine, *Word and Object* (1960), p. 36.

and transitivity. Thus, for instance, we say that "it is easily seen" (or "is obvious," or "is natural") that the relation of precedence is transitive, or that "n is divisible by 4" implies "n is divisible by 2" and not vice versa.[47] But no mysterious faculty of the soul is involved here; it is just a question of training, and those who lack it will not even understand what it is all about. And even experts are not always exempt from elementary fallacies, such as taking the single-arrow "If p, then q" for the double-arrow "p if and only if q."

Logical and semantic analysis contributes to the elucidation, or explication,[48] of rough, preanalytic, or intuitive terms. But in science this task of conceptual refinement is performed almost automatically alongside the theoretical elaboration; the theorification[49] of a concept, or of a statement, is the most common and probably the most effective way of refining it. It is only rarely that the scientist pauses to construct a careful definition of some key term. The meaning of a scientific term is best specified by the set of all law statements in which it occurs.

Ordinary language lacks a technique for deciding whether a given proposition actually follows from some other proposition. We remain content with an "intuitive" estimate—which may be false. Non sequitur, camouflaged with "hence," "thus," and kindred terms, is the most common logical weed of ordinary language. It is only by resorting to symbolic techniques that we may confidently attack the problem of proving the existence of a relation of deducibility. And in such a case we may arrive at counterintuitive results, that is, at propositions contradicting common sense.

But it must not be forgotten that elucidation is gradual. There are different levels of analysis and different degrees of refine-

[47] See Pap, *The Elements of Analytic Philosophy* (1949), p. 468.

[48] The term 'explication' was introduced in this sense by Whewell in *Novum Organum Renovatum* (1858), p. 30, and independently reintroduced by Carnap, *Logical Foundations of Probability* (1950), chap. i.

[49] The term "theorification," standing for the incorporation of a hypothesis in a theory or its expansion into a theory, is introduced and explicated in Bunge, "The Place of Induction in Science" (1960).

ment of arguments, and there is no evidence that the process of refinement may end, unless the concept in question, or even the inference pattern under consideration, be entirely dismissed. What is refined for the current mathematician may be intuitive for the logician. (As Bôcher said, "There is now, and there always will be room in the world for good mathematicians of every grade of precision." [50]) What happens is that a moment is reached when the process of refinement of concepts and demonstrations satisfies *our* standards of rigor, standards that may be superseded.

The analyst of the eighteenth century was content with "intuitive" considerations regarding curves generated by moving points, and the increase and decrease of physical properties. Then came the arithmetization of analysis, which eliminated every reference to physical entities and processes that had previously occurred in the definitions of infinitesimals and of limit, and which we still use in a preliminary, intuitive approach, as when we say that $1:x^2$ "increases" as x tends to 0, or that it approaches 0 with "increasing" x "more rapidly" than $1:x$ does. (Not being physical objects, numbers can neither grow nor shrink.)

Who knows what standards of rigor and techniques for improving rigor will be established in the future? The faith of the formalist in the complete formalization of theories and in the definitive obtainment thereby of absolute rigor has proved to be an illusion as great—but by far more fertile—as the faith of the intuitionist in the self-evidence of basic intuitions.

The role of intuition in science

It is time to attempt an evaluation of the role of intuition in science. The history of science is the biography of the successes and failures of the cognitive activity, which is empirical, intuitive, and rational in various ways. Nothing in that history

[50] Bôcher, "The Fundamental Conceptions and Methods of Mathematics" (1905), p. 135.

warrants the presumption that intellectual intuition, a form intermediary between sensibility and discursive reason, is superior either to experience or to alert thinking. Intuitions, even synoptic grasps, occur isolated from one another and are, therefore, sterile by themselves. At the very best, intuitions can be regarded—in the words of a distinguished meteorologist—as unformulated and untested theories.[51] Formulated theories alone, theories *stricto sensu,* that is, systems of propositions respecting some theory of logic, may bind intuitive concepts together and may refine them until exact and fertile concepts are obtained. Only in the bosom of theories do problems occur in clusters, so that the solution to one of them throws some light on related problems and, in turn, poses new problems in the same or in contiguous fields. And only within theories does the corroboration of one proposition entail the confirmation or the refutation of several other propositions. The decision about the adequacy of any idea, even a provisional decision, requires its previous analytical working out, and this is an exclusively rational procedure; if the idea happens to refer to the world, or to ourselves, it will also require empirical procedures. No intuition that escapes either procedure, rational and empirical, will be fruitful.

In science, intuition, along with analogy and induction, is regarded as a heuristic tool, as a guide and support of reasoning. As Rey Pastor said in connection with mathematics, intuition

> . . . leads us to guess or to forebode a multitude of properties we would never discover otherwise. Intuition serves as a guide in demonstrations, pointing to the way we must follow in order to attain perfect rigor . . . [but] in modern mathematics intuition is relegated to the role of guide without demonstrative power, even though it helps us in conceiving the rigorous demonstration.[52]

[51] Eady, "Climate," in Bates (Ed.), *The Earth and its Atmosphere* (1957), p. 114.
[52] Rey Pastor, *Introducción a la matemática superior* (1916), p. 64.

Furthermore, intuition does not occur manifestly in the very beginning of science where we have the statement of problems, the psychological origin of which is either a rational dissatisfaction or a practical need. Nor does intuition occur in the final presentation of theories. And intuition does not subdue logic in the constructive stage; it is an aspect of a complex process in which deduction and criticism are at least as important as inspiration.

The various forms of intuition resemble other forms of knowing and reasoning, in that they must be *controlled* if they are to be useful. Placed between sensible intuition and pure reason, intellectual intuition is fertile. But out of control it leads to sterility, as shown by the case of intuitionist philosophers, to whom we owe only harangues on the virtues of intuitions and the sins of reason but not a single partial truth attained with the help of the various philosophical intuitions, the existence of which they assert without proof.

In short, it would not make sense to deny the existence of intuitions of various kinds as interesting psychical phenomena. The negative result gained by ignoring their existence is that various pseudosciences monopolize an important sector of thinking. A constructive attitude toward the problem of intuition involves the following:

(*a*) a careful analysis of the many meanings of the term "intuition" and a parsimonious use of it;

(*b*) an empirical and theoretical analysis, in the context of scientific psychology, of this remarkable mixture of experience and reason;

(*c*) a refinement of the products of intuition by means of the elaboration of concepts and propositions that give precision to, subsume, and enrich the intuitive ones.

4

CONCLUSIONS

The following conclusions are suggested by the foregoing examination of intuition and intuitionism.

(1) *Intellectual intuition is a genus of psychical phenomena intermediate between sensible intuition and reason*—or shares in both. The varieties of intuition are of equal interest to the psychology of thinking, to the theory of knowledge, and to the theory of plausible (nondemonstrative) inference.

But the mere existence of this class of phenomena *poses* problems rather than solves them. To say, "It is intuitively seen that *p*," or "It is intuitively seen that *q* follows from *p*," does not settle the questions of the validation of *p* and the validity of the inference; moreover, it opens the question why certain persons, in given circumstances, find certain propositions and arguments intuitive.

And the existence of intuitions of many kinds does not prove the existence of a *method* for obtaining secure knowledge in a direct way. Also, it does not give anyone a right to proclaim an intuitionist philosophy, just as the undeniable existence and usefulness of analogy and induction do not suffice to prove the existence of an analogical or an inductive method conceived as a set of infallible and neatly stated rules of procedure for the obtainment of truth.

Besides, every theory is a rational construction, and if we wish to have an adequate *theory* of intuition we should not resort to philosophers who abuse reason. A consistent intuitionist will refuse to build a cogent theory of intuition; an example is Le Roy, who wrote that "intuition" is undefinable, and that only intuitions can be had of intuition.[1] An intuitionist, if he is consistent, will abstain from analyzing the word "intuition" and from studying its various designata. His own philosophy, which is antianalytic, will prevent him from doing this. To expect an intuitionist theory of intuition is as naïve as to expect a mystical theory of mystical communion, or a schizophrenic theory of schizophrenia. And as long as no scientific theory of the various sorts of intellectual intuition is available we should be sober in our use of the word "intuition," which —as an eighteenth century *philosophe* would have said—is too often but a name for our ignorance.

(2) *Intuition is fertile to the extent that it is refined and worked out by reason.* The products of intuition are rough to the point of uselessness: they must be elucidated, developed, complicated. The intuitive "lightning," the hunch, may be interesting if it occurs in the mind of an expert and if it is cleansed and inserted into a theory, or at least in a body of grounded beliefs. This is how our intuitions gain in clarity and scope. By being converted into formulated concepts and propositions, they can be analyzed, worked out, and logically tied to further conceptual constructions. Fruitful intuitions are those which are incorporated in a body of rational knowledge and thereby *cease* being intuitions.

In the historical evolution of every discipline, the "intuitive" or presystematic stage is the first. But this does not mean that in the beginning of every theory *only* intuitions are found and that they are altogether effaced by the theory's progressive formalization. In science there is no intuition without logic, although occasionally some ideas do "leap to the mind" in a state of full maturity[2]; and it is doubtful whether a definitive logical tidiness can ever be attained (see *The excluded middle,* Chap. 2). As in the case of hygiene, what is achieved in each stage is

[1] Le Roy, *La pensée intuitive* (1929), Vol. I, pp. 147-8.
[2] See Weil, "L'Avenir des mathématiques," in Le Lionnais (Ed.), *Les grands courants de la pensée mathématique* (1948), p. 317.

judged in accordance with the prevailing standards, which usually become more and more exacting.

(3) *The construction of abstract theories is accompanied by an almost complete elimination of intuitive elements.* The proliferation of abstract theories, consisting of signs lacking a fixed meaning, in logic as well as in mathematics, shows the fertility of discursive reason, which builds pure structures, such as pure spaces and pure groups, i.e., spaces and groups *tout court*, not spaces and groups *of* something. The elements or members of these structures have no fixed "nature" and, therefore, enable us to assign *a posteriori* a plurality of interpretations to the structures.[3] What matters in such theories are the relations among the elements rather than the elements themselves, which, except for the relations they satisfy, are entirely nondescript.

Such pure structures are not built intuitively, however, but, on the contrary, are constructed by eliminating, as much as possible, the intuitive content (arithmetical, geometrical, or kinematical) that is usually present in the original ideas, and by bringing into play counterintuitive "principles," such as the relation of isomorphism, or matching, among elements and relations of heterogeneous sets. Not intuition but pure reason can show the "essence" of the various abstract mathematical theories, because—however paradoxical or counterintuitive this may sound—what is essential to them is their logical form.

The mere existence of abstract theories shrinks the scope of intuition and refutes, incidentally, the thesis that every sign designates something. The realization that science uses signs without actual meanings—or, if preferred, with *potential meanings*—is critically important for an adequate appraisal of formal science and for a realization of the limitations of intuition. (On the other hand, it is obvious that *sensible* intuition is indispensable for the apprehension of the physical marks

---

[3] For a characterization of the notion of mathematical structure, see Bourbaki, "L'architecture des mathématiques," in the collective work mentioned in footnote 2.

representing the nondescript entities occurring in abstract theories.)

(4) *A similar elimination of intuitive elements accompanies the refinement of factual theories.* We have described above what can be called *semantically abstract* theories, that is, uninterpreted sign systems. But these constitute a subclass of a wider class, namely, that of *epistemologically abstract* theories, i.e., those theories containing concepts that are far from sense data, or terms that are not easily visualized. Every factual science has tended to achieve higher and higher degrees of epistemological abstraction as it converted given phenomena into problems to be solved. In this sense, the progress of factual science parallels that of mathematics: both become less and less intuitive.

It may be necessary to point out that epistemological abstractness does not necessarily involve lack of objective reference, i.e., semantical abstractness. Physical theories, however refined, are all *interpreted* systems (semantic systems), hence semantically nonabstract. But some theories are more sophisticated or elaborate than others, and contain a smaller number of visualizable concepts than the more "concrete" theories. Nobody has claimed that thermodynamics is a semantically abstract theory because its key concepts (state, temperature, energy, entropy) are largely unintuitive or because its diagrams are all nonfigurative, in the sense that they do not represent the motion of a system in spacetime.

(5) *Self-evidence is a psychological property of judgments and reasonings, not a logical property of propositions and inferences.* Consequently, (*a*) although the phenomenon of self-evidence or immediate clarity is psychologically and didactically interesting, it is epistemologically and logically irrelevant; no matter how it may be related to the *recognition* and *acceptance* of truth, it is not relevant either to the demonstration of truth or to the theory of truth, which must proceed apart from psychological and pragmatic considerations; (b) there exists no *objective*

criterion of full self-evidence, so that any decision to regard such and such a proposition as self-evident and, therefore, as fundamental or primitive is entirely arbitrary from a logical point of view;[4] (c) there are *degrees* of psychological self-evidence and logical rigor; the expert will regard as self-evident some arguments and propositions that may be simply unintelligible to the layman and will reject the latter's standards of rigor; (d) there is no justification whatever to continue identifying "self-evident" (a psychological category) with "axiomatic" (a metalogical term).

(6) *Self-evidence is neither necessary nor sufficient for the truth of a proposition or for the validity of an inference.* That self-evidence is not sufficient is empirically proved by the tall heap of nonsense that at some time or other has passed for intuitively self-evident.[5] That self-evidence is not necessary is shown by the fact that most of the high-level statements of factual science are far from self-evident, even to scientists in contiguous fields.

(7) *The premises of factual science may be suggested in various ways but are conclusively proved in none.* Analogy, induction, and possibly other forms of plausible inference as well, yield hypotheses, not secure truths; and before accepting such assumptions we must subject them to certain tests, both theoretical and empirical. Even then their acceptance will be provisional. If the hypotheses are adopted as postulates of some factual science, it is almost certain that in the long run they will have to be corrected or even altogether abandoned; and if the assumptions belong to formal science, the possibility should not be excluded that more comprehensive and fertile postulates may be found in the future. As to intellectual intui-

---

[4] A famous case was Brouwer's, who had stated that a certain theorem of Cantor's needed no demonstration because it was self-evident; five years later, he had to correct his statement, saying that the theorem in question was both non-self-evident and false. See Baldus, *Formalismus und Intuitionismus in der Mathematik* (1924), p. 33.

[5] For a survey of many such beliefs, see Evans, *The Natural History of Nonsense* (1946).

tion, e.g. geometrical or physical intuition, it no doubt has a heuristic value, but its probatory worth is nil, and it works only in the bosom of a body of knowledge.

(8) *Ultimate certainty and unshakeable foundation are not among the goals of scientific research,* even though few scientists resist the charm of such mirages. The progress of knowledge does not consist in a gradual removal of doubt and a corresponding gradual fixation of belief, but in posing new questions, or restating old problems in a new light, in offering provisional solutions to them with the help of more general and deeper theories and more powerful and precise techniques, and in creating new doubts. In science, as contrasted with dogma, for every removed doubt we gain several new questions. Scientific research is, therefore, neither fundamentalist nor infallibilist (see *Roots of Aristotelian intuitionism*, Chap. 1).

(9) *The occurrence of intuitions in science does not support intuitionism.* Scientific research is not a string of "visions" or judgments exempt from analysis and test. Creative scientists do have "natural revelations" or "illuminations," but never before finding, stating, and studying a *problem*. Hunches, global grasps, and other forms of intuition occur as a result of the careful analysis of problems, as a reward for patient and often obsessive preoccupation with them (see *Creative imagination,* Chap. 3).

Certainly the mere choice and formulation of a scientific or philosophic problem requires a dose of insight and sound judgment, or phronesis. Not everyone is capable of noticing the lacunae that must be filled, of correctly evaluating their importance, and of estimating the chances of successfully filling them. But scientists acquire such a "nose" after long experience. Besides, insight is not enough; hard work is necessary on most occasions to pose the problem in a convenient form, i.e., so that its solution may be attempted with the available means.

Between the recognition of a problem and its solution there are—in the psychological order—various stages: the preparation, or assimilation of relevant knowledge; the imagining and trial of various hypotheses; the synthesis that seems to solve the problem, and, finally, the test of the conjecture. All psychical dispositions, including the various kinds of intuition, take part in these stages.

(10) *Philosophical intuitionism, antianalytic and credulous, is opposed to the scientific spirit, which is essentially analytic and critical.* By postulating without any ground the existence of an extraordinary mode of cognition, higher than either experience or reason, the intuitionist philosopher saves himself the trouble of analyzing cognitive experience; by proclaiming the self-evidence of that which he intuitively "apprehends" (or, better, elaborates), he eludes criticism. In either case he kills the problem of knowledge instead of contributing to its solution.

Even mathematical intuitionism is philosophically naïve to the extent that it maintains the existence of unanalyzable (not further explicable) notions, namely, those which are intuitively given. When it is not a sign of candor—as it was in the case of the moderate intuitionism of traditional rationalists—philosophical intuitionism can be a pathological form of mental rigidity and conceitedness, as illustrated by Husserl, Scheler, and Heidegger.

Arrogant and dogmatic intuitionism, bordering on Messianism, seems to be a psychiatric disorder rather than a philosophical attitude. Only megalomaniacs are entitled to believe that they may "grasp" the entire truth without going through the process of ordinary experience and discursive reason, and only megalomaniacs believe that their own intuitions or illuminations are infallible.

(11) *Philosophical intuitionism is, in the best of cases, sterile.* It has produced no new knowledge and it never could yield it, because it is noncritical and antitheoretical, and because intuition is not an independent mode of knowing. Scientists and scientific philosophers do not thrive on sense data, intuitions, or eternal principles: problems, their solutions, and scrutable techniques for solving them are their nourishment.

And no important *problem* remains if the existence of a faculty is asserted, by means of which the essence of any object is directly and apodictically grasped.

Science, far from collecting intuitions, which are always vague, isolated, and unsafe, looks for problems and data and constructs theories and methods (instead of "apprehending" them). And the finding of problems, the gathering of data, the construction of nonspeculative theories, and the design and test of techniques, are frankly discouraged by intuitionism, which has a paralyzing effect on the so-called sciences of spirit.[6] To assign a scientific task to an intuitionist—who, if he is sincere, expects it all from an inner vision—would be as reasonable as assigning it to a gypsy or to a medium.

Scientific research is more and more a cooperative enterprise; it is social even when not performed by teams. What is social in scientific research is the public property (save some aberrant cases of secrecy) of problems, techniques, and results, as well as the public scrutiny of them. And such a social character of scientific work is challenged by intuitionism, which regards every thinker as a self-contained unit and values the ineffable and obscure over the communicable and clear.

(12) *At its worst, philosophical intuitionism is a dangerous variety of dogmatism.* Both in the development of the individual and in the evolution of culture, dogmatism, the uncritical acceptance of beliefs, comes first, and the critical approach comes last. Belief and its fixation come before doubt and test, which are traits of maturity. Critical cognition, characterized by an awareness of assumptions and limitations, as well as by a demand for test, is not found among children under eight; it is equally absent from much of everyday thinking, religion, and speculative philosophy. Among all the varieties of dogmatic philosophy intuitionism is the most dangerous, because it does not respect the instruments of *test*—reason and action—

---

[6] The paralyzing influence of philosophical intuitionism on Latin American sociology until recently has been pointed out by Germani, "The Development and Present State of Sociology in Latin America" (1959), p. 131.

that other philosophies admit. It is the only *self-validating* philosophy, needing neither argument nor evidence.

A product of mental laziness, ignorance, and superstition, child of a confusion between psychological self-evidence and epistemological and logical certainty, result of the untenable fundamentalist requirement, of the infallibilist prejudice, and of the unfulfillable wish of definitive security, philosophical intuitionism is a form of dogmatism far more dangerous for culture than aprioristic rationalism and sensist empiricism. It leads directly to authoritarianism, irrationalism, and charlatanism, the main enemies of cultural growth.

The following rules may be regarded as theoretically justified by the foregoing.

The word "intuition" should be used sparingly and, whenever possible, the kind of intuition referred to should be specified.

The most should be made out of sensible and intellectual intuition, by refining, expanding, and transcending their products in the light of theoretical knowledge.

No intuition should be left untested, and one's most deepseated intuitions should be revised from time to time.

Attention should be paid to the experimental frame of mind that characterizes mathematical intuitionism, not, however, to its epistemological naïveté and to its limitationist policy.

A cool critical eye should be kept on philosophical intuitionism, the chief foe of reason and a variety of quackery.

GLOSSARY

Abstract. A term is *epistemologically abstract* if it does not designate a sensible object, e.g., "number," "temperature." A term is *semantically abstract* if it is devoid of meaning, e.g., the terms of the abstract group theory.

Ad hominem argument. The rejection of a view because it is held by someone whom we disapprove of.

A fortiori. With stronger reason. (*The Concise Oxford Dictionary.*)

Algebraic number. Any number which is a solution of an alegebraic equation with integral coefficients. Thus $\sqrt{2}$ and $-\sqrt{2}$ solve the equation $x^2 - 2 = 0$; hence they are algebraic numbers.

Algorithm. Rule laying down the sequence of operations that must be performed in order to solve a special class of problems, such as the effective computation of a number or a function. Example: the standard procedure for extracting square roots.

Alternation. Disjunction of propositions ("p or q").

Analytic philosophy. In a broad sense, the class of philosophical trends which respect logic and emphasize the value of logical (syntactical and semantical) analysis. In a restricted sense, the philosophical school that makes the analysis of language its sole concern, with neglect of epistemology and ontology.

Analytic proposition. 1. In Kant's philosophy, a judgment is analytic if its predicate is "included" in its subject as, e.g., in "Composite systems are made up of less complex units." 2. In contemporary philosophy, a proposition that is true either by virtue of its logical form (e.g., "Not both p and not-p") or by virtue of the meaning of the constituent terms (e.g., "Water freezes at 0°C"). Usually, analytic propositions are not regarded as informative about facts. The propositions of logic and mathematics are all analytic. Antonym: *synthetic proposition.*

A priori. Prior to and independent of experience. Antonym: *a posteriori.* Logical and mathematical theorems are proved *a priori,* even though they may have been suggested, in a few cases, by experience.

Axiology. The theory of valuation.

Axiom. Statement taken as a starting point, or primitive (undemonstrated), in a given theory. Synonym: *postulate.*

Axiomatic theory. A theory expounded orderly, by first enumerating the primitive concepts and stating the primitive propositions (axioms).

Bourbaki, Nicolas. Collective pseudonym adopted by the brilliant *pléiede* of abstract mathematicians which includes H. Cartan, J. Dieudonné, L. Schwartz, and A. Weil.

Concept. Entity formed by the mind, and denoted by a term. E.g., the numeral "5" denotes the concept of the number five.

Conceptualism. The view that the units of discourse are concepts, and not mere marks (formalism) or faint reflections of transcendental Ideas (Platonism).

Convergence criteria. Rules that enable us to decide whether an infinite series converges to a finite value.

Decidable proposition. A proposition that can be shown to be true or false with the means provided by the system to which it belongs.

Deduction. Derivation of a statement from other statements in such a way that conclusion follows by virtue of the form or structure of the argument and apart from the meanings of the terms involved. Synonym: *deductive inference.*

Demonstrandum. The proposition that is to be demonstrated.

Diagonal procedures. Cantor's techniques for demonstrating the denumerability of rational numbers and the nondenumerability of real numbers.

Dichtung. German for poetry and, generally, for literature.

Dogmatism. Uncritical acceptance of beliefs.

Dynamicist. Emphasizing change.

Élan. French for drive or impetuosity. *Élan vital:* impulse of life, a key term in Bergson's philosophy.

Empathy. Understanding of other people's behavior by imagining oneself in their situation and without the help of science. Synonym: *sympathetic understanding.*

Empiricism. Class of philosophical theories holding that experience is the sole object, source, and test of knowledge. *Logical empiricism:* a modern version of empiricism, which recognizes the formal nature of logic and mathematics; synonym: *logical positivism.*

Entropy. A thermodynamic property related to bound energy (i.e., energy not available as work) and to degree of microscopic disorder in a macroscopic system. The second axiom of thermodynamics can be worded thus: "The entropy of an isolated system tends to increase." Or, alternatively, "The free energy of an isolated system tends to decrease."

Epistemology. Theory of knowledge. It deals with concepts such as those of perception, construction, proof, and guessing.

Euler-Venn's diagrams. Visual auxiliaries of the algebra of classes, whereby the latter are represented as circles on a plane. The sum of two classes is then represented as the entire region covered by the corresponding circles, and the product of two classes as the region common to the corresponding circles.

Existential statement. A statement beginning with the expressions "There exists," "There is at least one x such that," or cognates. The form of the simplest existential statement is "$(Ex)Px$," which is read as "There is at least one x such that x has the property P."

Existentialism. A variety of irrationalism dealing in an obscure and speculative way with being, nothingness, human existence, anguish, and other subjects usually treated by the sciences of man.

Explicandum. Term to be explicated or elucidated.

Explication. Elucidation and refinement of concepts. Definition, and incorporation into a theory (theorification), are usual procedures of explication.

Factual science. The set of disciplines dealing with concrete facts: physics, chemistry, biology, psychology, sociology, etc.

Fallibilism. The view that most of human knowledge is fallible, i.e., corrigible. Antonym: *infallibilism.*

Flatus vocis. Meaningless sound. Nominalism holds that every class term (e.g., "mankind") is a *flatus vocis,* i.e., a void term without reference.

Formalism. A trend in the philosophy of mathematics according to which (*a*) the objects of mathematics are physical signs, such as marks on paper; (*b*) the procedures of validation must involve a finite number of signs; and (c) logic is a branch of applied mathematics. The epistemology of formalism is nominalistic.

Formalization. A theory is said to be formalized if cast in axiomatic form and if, in addition, all its presuppositions and rules are explicitly stated.

Formal science. Nonfactual science, i.e., the set of disciplines dealing with conceptual entities with neglect of their possible reference. Formal science embraces logic and mathematics, as well as the corresponding metasciences.

Fourier integral. An integral of the form $\int_{-\infty}^{\infty} e^{itx} f(x)\, dx$.

Fundamentalism. The belief that every discipline must have an unassailable foundation.

Group. A set of elements subject to a rule of combination for uniting any pair of them and such that the combination of any two elements belongs to the set, the operation of combination obeys the associative law, every element has an inverse, and the set contains an identity element. If the nature of the elements and the operation are not specified, the group is said to be abstract.

Hermetic. Of occult "science."

Heuristic. Serving to discover. (*The Concise Oxford Dictionary.*) An important heuristic rule is "Vary the assumptions."

Hidden parameters. Variables not accessible to observation but supposed to describe the behavior of submicroscopic particles, whether they are under observation or free.

Historicism. The view that every human achievement is a step in a historical process.

Hypothesis. Corrigible proposition. The propositions of factual science are regarded by fallibilism as hypotheses even after corroboration.

Idealism. The set of philosophical schools according to which ideas are prior to things or, in other words, physical objects have no existence independent of some mind, whether human or divine.

Inclusion. A class *A* is included in a class *B* if and only if all the members of *A* belong also to *B*.

Induction. 1. In matters of fact, generalization from instances. 2. In mathematics, complete (or mathematical) induction is a technique of proof applicable to laws concerning or involving integers.

Inductivism. The belief that induction is the method of science, both for finding and testing laws.

Infallibilism. See *Fallibilism.*

Integration circuit. Line along which an integration is performed.

Iteration. Repeated application. Thus the repeated application of the operation "*a.*" yields a_n.

Lemma. A theorem proved for use in the proof of another theorem. (Glenn James and Robert C. James, *Mathematics Dictionary* [Princeton, New Jersey: Van Nostrand, 1959].)

Linear order. The order of a chain-like sequence. The order generated by the relation "less than" in the set of positive integers is linear. A linear order is *discrete* if the members of the sequence are denumerable.

Logicism. A trend in the philosophy of formal science according to which (*a*) propositions have a truth value whether or not they have been proved or disproved; (*b*) logic is prior to mathematics, and (*c*) the concepts of mathematics can all be constructed with the sole help of logical terms.

Ludic conception of mathematics. The conception according to which mathematical work is a game with marks or concepts, subject to arbitrary rules.

Materialism. The set of philosophical trends according to which everything is either material or a function of matter; in particular, mind is a function of the nervous system. A variety of naturalism.

Matrix. An array of elements (e.g., numbers). Determinants, which have a definite value, are formed out of matrices.

Metascience. The theory of science, embracing both the methodology and the philosophy of science.

Modus ponens. A basic rule of inference of the propositional calculus, according to which if a conditional ("If p then q") and its antecedent ("p") are both asserted, then the consequent ("q") can be asserted or detached.

Modus tollens. The rule of deductive inference enabling us to reject a proposition p if it implies a proposition q that is found to be false.

Naturalism. The class of philosophical trends that deny the existence of supernatural entities, and assert the natural evolution of life and mind out of physical units.

Nested intervals. A sequence of intervals, such as line segments, is called nested if each interval is contained in the preceding.

Nominalism. The view that concepts and propositions are only words or sounds, and that individuals alone have real existence. Mathematical and logical nominalism = formalism.

Non-zero matrix. A matrix the elements of which are not all zero. See *Matrix.*

Observation statement. A sentence describing an observation or expressing the result of an observation. According to empiricism, observation statements are the basic units of scientific discourse.

Operationalism. The branch of pragmatism holding that only operations can confer meanings upon terms, and that all scientific terms ought to be defined with reference to operations. On this view, "actual infinity," "mind," and "unobserved atom" are meaningless terms.

Orthogonal functions. Functions the scalar product of which is zero. Two functions, $f(x)$ and $g(x)$, are orthogonal to each other in a domain D if $(f,g) =_{df} \int_D \bar{f}(x)g(x)dx = 0$.

Paradox. 1. Statement leading to contradiction. "The statement I am now writing down is false" is one of the so-called paradoxes of self-reference. 2. Pseudoparadox (vide).

Photon hypothesis. The hypothesis, belonging to the quantum theory of radiation, that the energy of a light wave consists of discrete units (quanta).

Platonism. 1. In epistemology, the view that ideas preëxist things and the latter are imperfect copies of the former. 2. In the philosophy of mathematics, the view espoused by logicism—that propositions are true or false whether or not they have been verified, so that the act of demonstration is a discovery rather than a creation.

Postulate. Axiom.

Pragmatic analysis. The branch of semiotics dealing with the use of terms and the occasions and motives for their use. Synonym: *pragmatics.*

Pragmatism. The philosophical school according to which action is both the source and the test of all knowledge, and terms that do not somehow denote action are meaningless.

Proposition. The logical correlate of the judgment, in turn a psychological entity. Formalists and pragmatists prefer to speak of *sen-*

tences or *statements*. Conceptualists would hold that statements are the linguistic expression of propositions.

Protocol statement. A sentence, couched in sense-data language, and describing an observation. E.g., "Here now I feel a red patch." Science has no use for such primitive and subjective utterances.

Positivism. A kind of empiricism, characterized by the emphasis on sense data and induction, the acceptance of the descriptive parts of science, a certain distrust of theory, and the refusal to admit the reality of the physical world. See *empiricism*.

Presystematic thinking. Thinking that does not take place within the framework of a conceptual system (theory).

Probability cloud. The image of a probability distribution of position. In quantum theory, the position of a fairly well localized particle may be pictured as a small cloud the density of which corresponds to the probability that the particle occupies a given place within the cloud.

Pseudoparadox. Statement incompatible with current opinion, whether popular or scientific.

Psychologism. The tendency to equate logical entities with psychological operations.

Pythagorean participation. The view that everything participates in everything else.

Rationalism. In a broad sense, the set of philosophies which trust reason. In a strict sense, the set of philosophies which maintain that pure reasoning suffices for both formal and factual science; synonym: *traditional rationalism*.

Realism. 1. Objectivism, i.e., the view that the external world exists by itself, without some mind perceiving or thinking it. The opposite of idealism. 2. *Platonic realism:* the doctrine that ideas exist prior to men and are even more real than things, which in turn are nothing but defective copies of ideas. A variety of idealism.

Reification. Conversion of a property, function, or abstract term, into a thing or agent. E.g., in "Intuition makes us grasp the essence of things," intuition is treated as a separate thing, i.e., it is reified.

Rules of designation. Semantical rules that lay down the meaning of signs. E.g., " '*p*' denotes a propositional variable."

Rules of formation. Syntactical rules that lay down the possible correct ways of combining signs. E.g., "The sign standing for the product of two elements must occur between the elements."

Rules of transformation. Syntactical rules that lay down the inferences that can be drawn from given statements. E.g., the rule of substitution and the *modus ponens*.

Scattering graph. A diagram picturing an elementary event such as the collision of an electron with a photon. Synonym: *Feynman's graph*.

Semantic system. A system of signs, such as a natural language, or a factual theory, all of them endowed with some meaning. Antonyms: *abstract system, uninterpreted system*.

Semantics. The study of the relations among signs and their designata, if any, as well as of their epistemic status. The concepts of denotation, meaning, analyticity, and truth, are all semantic.

Semiotics. The theory of signs, embracing syntax, semantics and pragmatics.

Sense data. Information provided by sense perception.

Sensism. The view that no term is meaningful unless it describes a sense datum or a complex of sense experiences.

Sequence. A set of terms ordered like the set of positive integers. Not to be confused with *series*, which is a sum of terms, usually an infinite sum.

Set theory. The theory of infinite sets. Characteristic set-theoretical concepts are the relations "belongs to" and "is included in." Almost the entire body of mathematics can now be built with the sole help of logic and set theory.

Shell nuclear model. The theory, and the accompanying visual model, according to which the particles in an atomic nucleus are arranged in shells similar to the extranuclear electronic shells.

Singular statement. A statement in which only logical constants occur. E.g., "$2 + 1 = 3$," and "This book is puzzling."

Speculative philosophy. The class of philosophical trends that do not care for the test of the hypotheses they advance, e.g., hegelianism and existentialism.

Spin hypothesis. The hypothesis that elementary particles, such as the electron and the proton, possess a quantum-mechanical property the classical analogue of which is the intrinsic angular rotation.

Syntactic. Of syntax.

Syntax. The study of the relations among signs without caring for their meaning and use, if any.

Synthetic judgment. 1. In Kant's philosophy, a judgment is synthetic if its predicate is not "included" in its subject, as, e.g., in "Argentina is a civilized country." 2. In contemporary philosophy, a proposition that cannot be validated *a priori,* but is true or false by virtue of facts. Antonym: *analytic proposition.*

Theorem. Statement derivable from other statements of a theory.

Theorification. A hypothesis is theorified if included in, or expanded into, a theory.

Theory. A system of propositions that refer to some subject matter, so that its propositions are either independent from one another (axioms) or are connected through the relation of entailment, and so that the concepts occurring in the propositions somehow hang together.

Transcendental number. A number which is not a root of an algebraic equation with integral coefficients; e.g., *e* and π.

Transform away. The motion of a body can be transformed away by rigidly attaching the reference system to the body.

Transitivity. A relation "*R*" such that, if *xRy* and *yRz*, then *xRz*, is called transitive. The relations of equality and inequality are transitive; the relation of similarity is intransitive.

Tree. A visualization of logical operations. The logical formula "*p* or *q*" is pictured thus:

$\underline{p}$ or $\underline{q}$

$\underline{p}$ $\underline{q}$

The formula "*P(x)*," in the universe of integers ($x = 1, 2, 3, \ldots n,$ . . .), is pictured in this way:

$\underline{P}(1)$

$\underline{P}(2)$

$\underline{P}(3)$

etc.

Truth. 1. *Formal truth:* A proposition is formally true either by convention or because it is entailed by previously accepted premises. 2. *Factual truth:* A proposition is factually true of it describes or refers to an actual state of affairs in an accurate way.

Undecidable proposition. A proposition that cannot be formally derived in a given system, even though it may be recognized as true or false in a semi-rigorous way or with the help of stronger rules of inference.

Universal statement. A statement beginning with the words "all" or "for all." The form of the simplest universal statement is "$(x)Px$", i.e., "For all x, x is a P."

Variable. 1. In formal science, that which may take on as values entities with a fixed meaning. Examples: the individual variables "x", "y", etc., and the propositional variables "p", "q", etc. 2. In factual science, a concept denoting a property of a concrete system. Examples: "position" and "solubility."

Wahrheit. German for truth.

Wave packet. A bundle of infinite monochromatic waves with slightly different frequencies. Synonym: *wave group.*

BIBLIOGRAPHY

When two dates are given the first refers to the original publication.

Aristotle. *Posterior Analytics*, in *The Basic Works of Aristotle*. Edited by R. McKeon. New York: Random House, 1941.

Baldus, Richard. *Formalismus und Intuitionismus in der Mathematik.* Karlsruhe: Braun, 1924.

Bartlett, Frederic C. "The Relevance of Visual Imagery to the Process of Thinking," *British Journal of Psychology* (London: George Allen & Unwin Ltd.), XVIII (1927), 23.

——————. *Thinking: An Experimental and Social Study*. New York: Basic Books, 1958.

Bates, D. R. (ed.). *The Earth and Its Atmosphere*. New York: Basic Books. 1957.

Baylis, C. A. "Are Some Propositions Neither True Nor False?", *Philosophy of Science*, III (1936), 157.

Bergson, Henri. "Introduction à la métaphysique," *Revue de métaphysique et de morale*, XI (1903), 1.

——————. *L'évolution créatrice* (1907). Paris: Presses Universitaires de France, 1948.

——————. "L'intuition philosophique," *Revue de métaphysique et de morale*, XIX (1911), 809.

Bernard, Claude. *Introduction à l'étude de la médecine expérimentale* (1865). Paris: Flammarion, 1952.

Beth, E. W. "Semantic Construction of Intuitionist Logic," *Mededelingen der Koninklijke Nederlandse Akademie van Wettenschappen*, Afd. Letterkunde, N. S., XIX, No. 11 (1956), 357.

——————. "*Cogito ergo sum*—raisonnement ou intuition?" *Dialectica*, XII (1958), 223.

Black, Max. *The Nature of Mathematics*. London: Routledge & Kegan Paul, 1933.

Bôcher, Maxime. "The Fundamental Conceptions and Methods of Mathematics," *Bulletin of the American Mathematical Society*, XI (1905), 115.

Borel, Emile. "Logique et intuition en mathématiques," *Revue de métaphysique et de morale,* XV (1907), 273.

Bridgman, P. W. *Reflections of a Physicist.* New York: Philosophical Library, 1955.

Brouwer, L. E. J. "Intuitionism and Formalism," *Bulletin of the American Mathematical Society,* XX (1913), 81.

Bunge, Mario. "La fenomenología y la ciencia," *Cuadernos Americanos* (México), X, No. 4 (1951), 108.

——————————. *Metascientific Queries.* Springfield, Ill.: Charles C. Thomas, 1959.

——————————. *Causality: The place of the Causal Principle in Modern Science.* Cambridge, Mass.: Harvard University Press, 1959.

——————————. "The Place of Induction in Science," *Philosophy of Science,* XXVII (1960), 262.

——————————. *Etica y ciencia* (Buenos Aires: Siglo Veinte, 1960).

——————————. "The Weight of Simplicity in the Construction and Assaying of Scientific Theories," *Philosophy of Science,* XXVIII (1961), 120.

——————————. "Ethics as a Science," *Philosophy and Phenomenological Research,*

——————————. "A Mathematical Theory of Partial Truth" (forthcoming).

Cannon, Walter B. *The Way of an Investigator.* New York: Norton, 1945.

Carnap, Rudolf. "Die logizistische Grundlegung der Mathematik," *Erkenntnis,* II (1931), 91.

——————————. *Foundations of Logic and Mathematics,* in *International Encyclopedia of Unified Science.* Vol. I, No. 3, Chicago: University of Chicago Press, 1939.

——————————. *Logical Foundations of Probability.* Chicago: The University of Chicago Press, 1950.

Cobb, Stanley. *Foundations of Neuropsychiatry.* 5th ed. Baltimore: Williams & Wilkins, 1952.

Courant, Richard, and Robbins, Herbert. *What is Mathematics?* London: Oxford University Press, 1941.

Couturat, Louis. *Les principes des mathématiques.* Paris: Alcan, 1905.

——————————. "Logistique et intuition," *Revue de métaphysique et de morale,* XXI (1913), 260.

Curry, Haskell B. *Outlines of a Formalist Philosophy of Mathematics.* Amsterdam: North-Holland, 1951.

Denjoy, Arnaud. "Rapport général," *Congrès International de Philosophie des Sciences* (Paris, 1949). Paris: Hermann, 1951.

Descartes, René. *Oeuvres.* Edited by V. Cousin. Paris: Levrault, 1824-26.

Dewey, John. *Essays in Experimental Logic* (1916). New York: Dover, 1953.

Dieudonné, Jean. "L'axiomatique dans les mathématiques modernes," *Congrès International de Philosophie des Sciences* (Paris, 1949). Paris: Hermann, 1951, III.

Dilthey, Wilhelm. *Gesammelte Werke.* Leipzig-Berlin: Teubner, 1923.

Dubos, René J. *Louis Pasteur, Free Lance of Science.* Boston: Little, Brown, 1950.

Eady, E. T. "Climate," in *The Earth and its Atmosphere.* Edited by D. R. Bates. New York: Basic Books, 1957.

Evans, Bergen. *The Natural History of Nonsense* (1946). New York: Vintage Books, 1959.

Ewing, A. C. "Reason and Intuition," *Proceedings of the British Academy,* XXVII (1941).

Feigl, Herbert, and Brodbeck, May. *Readings in the Philosophy of Science.* New York: Appleton-Century-Crofts, 1953.

Frank, Philipp. *Modern Science and its Philosophy.* Cambridge, Mass.: Harvard University Press, 1949.

Freud, Sigmund. *A General Introduction to Psychoanalysis* (1924). New York: Washington Square Press, 1960.

Freudenthal, Hans. "Le développement de la notion d'espace depuis Kant," *Sciences,* No. 3 (1959).

Germani, Gino. "The Development and Present State of Sociology in Latin America," *Transactions of the Fourth World Congress of Sociology* (London: International Sociological Association, 1959), Vol. I.

Goodman, Nelson. *Fact, Fiction, & Forecast.* London: Athlone Press, 1954; Cambridge, Mass.: Harvard University Press, 1955.

Hadamard, Jacques. *The Psychology of Invention in the Mathematical Field* (1945). New York: Dover, 1954.

Hahn, Hans. "The Crisis of Intuition" in *The World of Mathematics.* Edited by J. R. Newman. New York: Simon & Schuster, 1956.

Hartmann, Nicolai. *Einführung in die Philosophie.* 3rd. ed. Osnabrück: Luise Hanckel, 1954.

Heyting, A. "Die intuitionistische Grundlegung der Mathematik," *Erkenntnis,* II (1931), 106.

—————. *Intuitionism: An Introduction.* Amsterdam: North-Holland, 1956.

—————. "La conception intuitionniste de la logique," *Les études philosophiques,* XI (1956), 226.

—————. "Intuitionism in Mathematics" in Vol. I of *Philosophy in the Mid-Century.* Edited by R. Klibansky. Firenze: La Nuova Italia, 1958.

————— (ed.). *Constructivity in Mathematics: Proceedings of the Colloquium held at Amsterdam, 1957.* Amsterdam: North-Holland, 1959.

Hilbert, David. *Grundlagen der Geometrie* (1899). 7th ed. Leipzig-Berlin: Teubner, 1930.

—————. "Über das Unendliche," *Mathematische Annalen,* XCV (1925), 161.

—————, and Cohn-Vossen, S. *Anschauliche Geometrie.* Berlin: Springer, 1932.

Husserl, Edmund. *Husserliana.* Haag: Martinus Nijhoff, 1950.

—————. *Philosophie der Arithmetik.* Leipzig: Haacke, 1891.

—————. *Ideas: General Introduction to Pure Phenomenology.* Translated by W. R. Boyce Gibson. London: Allen & Unwin, 1931.

James, William. *Essays in Radical Empiricism and A Pluralistic Universe* (1909). New York: Longmans, Green, 1958.

Kant, Immanuel. *Kritik der reinen Vernunft* (1781, 1787). Edited by R. Schmidt. Hamburg: Meiner, 1952. Translated by N. Kemp Smith. *Immanuel Kant's Critique of Pure Reason.* London: Macmillan, 1929.

Klein, Felix. *Elementary Mathematics from an Advanced Standpoint* (1911-14). 2 vols. New York: Macmillan, 1932 and 1939.

Klemm, Friedrich. *A History of Western Technology.* Translated by D. Waley Singer. New York: Charles Scribner's Sons, 1959.

Koch, Sigmund (ed.). *Psychology: A Study of a Science.* Vol. II. New York: McGraw-Hill, 1959.

Kolnai, Aurel. *The War Against the West.* London: Gollancz, 1938.

Le Roy, Edouard. *La pensée intuitive.* 2 vols. Paris: Boivin, 1929 and 1930.

Libby, Walter. "The Scientific Imagination," *Scientific Monthly,* XV (1922), 263.

Le Lionnais, F. (ed.). *Les grands courants de la pensée mathématique.* Paris: Les Cahiers du Sud, 1948.

Luneburg, Rudolf K. *Mathematical Analysis of Binocular Vision.* Princeton: Princeton University Press, 1947.

Mach, Ernst. *Erkenntnis und Irrtum.* Leipzig: Barth, 1905.

McKellar, Peter. *Imagination and Thinking.* London: Cohen & West, 1957.

Margenau, Henry. "Phenomenology and Physics," *Philosophy and Phenomenological Research,* V (1944), 269.

Mises, Richard von. *Positivism: A Study in Human Understanding.* Cambridge, Mass.: Harvard University Press, 1951.

Moore, G. E. *Principia Ethica* (1903). Cambridge University Press, 1959.

Nagel, Ernest, and Newman, James R. *Gödel's Proof.* New York: New York University Press, 1958.

Neumann, Johann von. "Die formalistische Grundlegung der Mathematik," *Erkenntnis,* II (1931), 116.

Osgood, Charles E. *Method and Theory in Experimental Psychology.* New York: Oxford University Press, 1953.

Pap, Arthur. *Elements of Analytic Philosophy.* New York: Macmillan, 1949.

Pederson-Krag, Geraldine. "The Use of Metaphor in Analytic Thinking," *Psychoanalytic Quarterly,* XXV (1956), 66.

Peirce, Charles S. *Values in a Universe of Chance.* Edited by P. Wiener. New York: Doubleday, 1958.

Piaget, Jean. *The Psychology of Intelligence.* New York: Harcourt, Brace & Co., 1950.

Platt, Washington, and Baker, Ross A. "The Relation of the Scientific 'Hunch' to Research," *Journal of Chemical Education,* VIII (1931), 1969.

Poincaré, Henri. *La valeur de la science.* Paris: Flammarion, 1906.

———. *Science et méthode.* Paris: Flammarion, 1908.

Polya, G. *Mathematics and Plausible Reasoning.* 2 vols. Princeton: Princeton University Press, 1954.

Popper, Karl R. *The Logic of Scientific Discovery* (1935). London: Hutchinson, 1959.

———. "On the Sources of our Knowledge," *Indian Journal of Philosophy,* I, 3 (1959).

Quine, Willard V. *From a Logical Point of View.* Cambridge, Mass.: Harvard University Press, 1953.

———. *Word and Object.* New York: The Technological Press of the M.I.T. and Wiley, 1960.

Reichenbach, Hans. *The Philosophy of Space and Time* (1928). New York: Dover Publications, Inc., 1958.

Rey Pastor, Julio. *Introducción a la matemática superior*. Madrid: Biblioteca Corona, 1916.

Ribot, Théodule. *Essai sur l'imagination créatrice*. Paris: Alcan, 1900.

Russell, Bertrand. *Mysticism and Logic* (1918). London: Penguin Books, 1953.

——————. "On Vagueness," *Australasian Journal of Psychology and Philosophy*, I (1923). 84.

Scheler, Max. *Der Formalismus in der Ethik und die materiale Wertethik* (1916). Bern: Francke, 1954.

Schiller, F. C. S. "Hypothesis," in Vol. II of *Studies in the History and Method of Science*. Edited by C. Singer. Oxford: Clarendon Press, 1921.

Schlick, Moritz. *Allgemeine Erkenntnislehre*. 2nd. ed. Berlin: Springer, 1925.

Sellars, Roy Wood, McGill, J., and Farber, Marvin, (eds.). *Philosophy for the Future*. New York: Macmillan, 1949.

Spinoza, Baruch. *Ethique*, bilingual text. Translated by Ch. Appuhn. Paris: Garnier, 1909.

Springbett, B. M., Dark, J. G., and Clake, J., "An Approach to the Measurement of Creative Thinking," *Canadian Journal of Psychology*, XI (1957), 9.

Stern, Alfred. "Significado de la fenomenología," *Minerva* (Buenos Aires), I (1944), 197.

——————. "Max Scheler, filósofo de la guerra total y del estado totalitario," *Minerva*, II (1945), 109.

Struik, Dirk J. "Mathematics," in *Philosophy for the Future*. Edited by Roy Wood Sellars *et al.* (New York: Macmillan, 1949).

Suppes, Patrick. *Introduction to Logic*. Princeton: Van Nostrand, 1957.

Tarski, Alfred. *Logic, Semantics, Metamathematics*. Translated by J. H. Woodger. Oxford: Clarendon Press, 1956.

Taylor, Donald W., Berry, Paul C., and Block, Clifford H. "Does Group Participation when Using Brainstorming Facilitate or Inhibit Creative Thinking?" *Administrative Science Quarterly*, III (1958), 23.

Waismann, Friedrich. *Introduction to Mathematical Thinking* (1951). New York: Harper & Brothers, 1959.

Wertheimer, Max. *Productive Thinking*. New York and London: Harper and Brothers, 1945.

Weyl, Hermann. *Philosophy of Mathematics and Natural Science* (1927). Princeton: Princeton University Press, 1949.

Whewell, William. *History of the Inductive Sciences.* 3rd. ed. 2 vols. New York: Appleton, 1858.

——————. *Novum Organum Renovatum.* 3rd. ed. London: Parker, 1858.

Wilder, Raymond L. *Introduction to the Foundations of Mathematics* (New York: Wiley, 1952).

Zilsel, Edgar. "Phenomenology and Natural Science," *Philosophy of Science,* VIII (1941), 26.

INDEX